a map of sorts

John K. Lawson has roots in Plymouth, England and in the USA. A visual artist with work in many private and public collections internationally, he is also a published poet and novelist. His two previous books, *Figures in Jazz* and *Maker Rebirth*, both combine his poetry and visual art in provocative dialogue with each other. His poetry is published regularly in the Berkshire Edge, in the USA. Following the success of his first collection of poems, *NOW*, published by Westwords Press in 2014, *A Map of Sorts* continues John's exploration of what it means to be human in the 21st century.

By the same author

Hurricane Hotel
Figures in Jazz
NOW
Maker Rebirth

Acknowledgements

Some of these poems where first published in The Berkshire Edge.

My warm thanks to Jon West-Bey , Chairman and Founder of the Poetry Museum, Washington DC; Kelly Gartman; Cathy Galvin; Ann Grey; Nancy Franco; and Aimee K. Michel for keeping the flame blazing; Francis Mallett; and Mark Penwill for adding his magic touch.

Front cover Image: *NO Man's Land* by JK Lawson.
Salvaged flood damaged drawings, encaustic, ink.
2008, 36 x 44 x 2 ins. Collection of the artist.

a map of sorts

j k lawson

Second Edition

First published in Great Britain in 2016 by White Lane Press, Plymouth.

Copyright © John K Lawson 2016

The right of John K Lawson to be identified as the author of this work has been asserted by him in accordance with the Copyright, Designs and Patents Act of 1988.

All rights reserved.

ISBN 978-0-9568488-6-4

a map of sorts

Introduction

I know the poet – and artist – John K. Lawson as Some Guy Upstairs. I'm the Other Guy Upstairs.

For a number of years, when he's on this side of the Atlantic, he and I have worked in the same building in the center of Great Barrington, a small town in the Berkshire mountains of Western Massachusetts, an epicenter of a cultural activity, where the woods are alive with dancers, writers, actors, musicians and artists.

I'm the editor of an online newspaper, The Berkshire Edge, that relies upon JK for poetic interpretation of what is happening both in our corner of the world as well as on the world stage, or from wherever JK happens to be – New Orleans, England, Logan Airport in Boston. I would open my email, and there would be an urgent message alerting me that a poem, and accompanying illustration, would soon be on its way.

And shortly would arrive a passionate statement in verse about the terrorist attack in Paris, or the Brexit vote in England, or the death of David Bowie, the demise of a proposal to upgrade the local high school, the terrorist shootings in San Bernardino, or the opioid epidemic that has insinuated itself into the lives of so many people, young and old, neighbours and friends, even in our rural community; an affliction that JK knows from personal experience and summoned in his poem *Overdose*. Accompanying his poems would be an extraordinary collage that fashioned a visual reference.

His poems – and his art – have developed an attentive following. Readers know what he is talking about. In this sense, Lawson is in the tradition of being a public poet, finding poetic inspiration in commonly beheld occurrences, as W.B. Yeats did in his poems about Irish aspiration for independence.

But in addition, the poems in this collection, Lawson's second, do indeed create 'a map of sorts', the title of this volume. Lawson is the cartographer of our fractalized existence, where the role of the poet is to piece together, as best he can, fragments of images, of associations, of language – the scraps and ribbons and threads of a shredded fabric of reality – in the hope of creating a delay in the onslaught of chaos.

David Scribner, 2016.

Contents

a map of sorts

a map of sorts	*page 14*
1977	*16*
brentor	*17-18*
black out versus day dream	*19-21*
beehive	*22-23*
bead lady	*24-26*
happy cabbies take a smoke break	*27*
found objects	*28*
brawling between two black eyes	*29*
elvis is driving this crate	*30-31*
saints to go	*32*
hey slugger	*33-34*
crazy george	*35*
ghost rats	*36-37*
labor day	*38*
blood brothers	*39*
3am feels smooth	*40-42*
merry magdalene	*43-44*
no matter what	*45*
what is a town without a sound	*46-47*
coffin maker	*48*
gutter punks	*49-50*
clawing into a dream	*51*
francine	*52*
whispers lap his feet	*53*
rain preacher	*54-55*
pay back	*56*
cash flow	*57*
helicopters	*58-59*
skew whiff sockets jam na na beats	*60-61*
chaucer	*62-63*
mona always knew	*64*
almost alone	*65*
knocked out with a head cold	*66-67*

dizzy echoes of tomorrow

dizzy echoes of tomorrow	*page 70-72*
inside a william coleridge dream	*73*
message received	*74*
avocados sound like hand grenades	*75-76*
downtown houston	*77*
dagger dodge and his sharpie logic	*78*
last seen wearing the rags of his own undoing	*79-81*
in passing	*82*
letters written	*83*
nurse bertie	*84*
blood sports	*85*
see how she sleeps	*86*
old man darwin	*87*
shiny white teeth	*88*
following the footsteps of ghosts	*89*
the slog of ink	*90*
on this feisty carnival parade	*91*
hunter	*92*
under the shade of any old moon	*93-95*
vaccine city	*96-99*
savannah	*100-01*
myth	*102*
breathe	*103*
as long as i pay the antitheist today	*104-05*
burnt out star	*106-07*
clear skies and chap stick	*108*
spinning with the ways of the sun	*109*
fossil onlooker	*110-11*
odours haunt me	*112*
christmas tree	*113*
squeeze the dream	*114*
mickey mouse is weeping	*115-16*
in the crystal night of knowing	*117-18*
two pressure cookers	*119*
zapatista	*120*

going up in flames	*121*
jarret	*122*
mister keys	*123*
will she	*124-25*
what falls thru the night	*126-27*
without reason	*128*
beware the toes you step on today	*129-30*
one sin is as good as any other	*131-32*
strange unfriendly places	*133*
sticky sweet cactus	*134-35*
whistle blower	*136-37*
bugs burn in the lamp	*138-39*
us three	*140-41*
lifer	*142*
the brightest light can shine in the darkest places	*143-44*
thalia	*145*
when dreams are reality	*146*
crack on	*147-49*
zippo slaves	*150*
ode to blakes mandible	*151*
without words	*152*

skin mates

skin mates	*page 154-56*
oh sad country of my bones	*157-60*
blowing burnt ash onto tepid ink	*161*
i chart these poems onto your skin	*162*
later	*163*
shadow	*164*
disco donny	*165-66*
squiggles in the rain	*167-68*
al green is playing on the radio	*169-70*

overdose

overdose	*page 172-79*
now where	*180*
impossible star	*181*
the sacred drizzle of acceptance	*182-83*
exact size	*184*
from the beginning	*185-87*
bombs are dropping there	*188*
where we are	*189*
cake walk	*190*
beneath the skin	*191*
hanging with quasimodo vultures	*192*
keep on keeping on	*193*
a slash of reddish polka dots	*194-95*
an omen of sorts	*196*
far rockaway beach	*197-98*
enough will never do	*199-200*
holding hands	*201*
backfire	*202*
no matter what	*203*
buried alive	*204*
laced in splinters	*205*
make the distance	*206*

all that floats feels raw

all that floats feels raw	*page 208*
he began to notice	*209*
outside harrys	*210-11*
crawling back into itself	*212*
a world on fire	*213-15*
late again yet feeling early	*216*
tomorrows old news	*217-18*
another stinger down	*219*
token	*220*
travelling the distance between pen and ink	*221*
someone other than me	*222*

*for Elizabeth Nell Dubus
and the spirit of Cajuns everywhere*

a map of sorts

a map of sorts

woken in a cold sweat
barely living in a sweating town

gun shots from the next block
ricochet off building walls

echoes of the way we are
filter along unlit corridors

broken windows reflect dead end streets
freshly painted with double yellow lines

i fumble for a lighter a cigarette a pen
and someone like you to scratch on

writing poetry is the ignited wings
busting open barbed wire cages

writing poetry lives on within
these contaminated flames

*

sharp shadows bite back
if only we can rub ourselves clean

yet nothing it seems can be found
itching raw on bended knees

in our collapsible room
where polka dots and purple stains

create a map of sorts
on your bleached out skin

a map of where we are most likely going
or worse a premonition of what we have already seen

in this vast unrecognizable space
filled with speechless hours listening to endless gunshots

trying to figure out how on earth
given what we already know and have

can we ever really learn
to forgive ourselves

1977

seconds squeeze out of the pubs
following bricks thrown and stones

clouds of gas disperse fresh riots
on the streets of a brixton sun

tombs of bathroom walls disband and reassemble
a pre zombie youth awaiting the first bite

with fresh ink and pale skin these gin pissed poets
know well enough not to read the news

as feelings brew tired from being raped
and misguided by adult problems

rusty safety pins and a stinking garbage truck
filled to the brim with a pack of skinny unfixable scars

littered with vacant eyes
record searing vocabularies

in basements and abandoned garages
already consumed with flames

brentor

imagine an island
a hole in the bucket island
where warmth can be found for the traveller sleep
chained to rocks and imprisoned by a sea
kissed with razor bracken surf
crashing in granite waves

etched in tides
weather beaten with time
a walk on water miracle
on high kite level

clouds creak above this ocean
as if following ancient footsteps
the suns humour freckles with shadows
across ageless cast offs
worn in the sublime
creating a reference point
and escape for many

opening up a chance for no turning back
through lanes clinging to themselves
beaten away by a silence
like dew trapped in a web
or bony willow fingers
scraping down a dusty school board
laced with chalk drawn sheep
their absent eyes gazing through heads
chipped and chewing on clusters

brentor
pricked in purple shades
and flickering blues
your sharp edges are words
in the thorn stick fields fading into hedgerows

time can be heard entangled in time riddled songs
gift wrapped with moments like well worn lovers
lost in the misty depths of autumn conversation

slippery veins wet with streams
roll over this land like an open wound
torn and bruised and rough skinned
as the crumbling chapel cries to permit
a pinnacle of belief to rise within

carrion banished from laughter
guard the initials etched on tombstones
hugging grave reminders to all who venture here
life has domain in forgotten traces

brentor
dusk opens up as a lip stick mouth
speaking in tongues flames of clouds
flicker scorched tails in a turner landscape
where tethered hearts descend
after the fulfilment for flight left them
accepting a two hour climb up
can become a three mile landslide down
creating a friendship of sorts
like a strangers greeting
without pressure or strain
before a chance to return
across sheep stained fields
connects these ship wrecked survivors
afloat in the dartmoor mist

black out versus day dream

and there you are neatly framed in
a greying photograph featuring

a sauced james joyce
evicted from a nameless foreign bar

gathered in gratitude until the worst happens
and chairs are left unfolded

seconds become hours filled in
with prescriptions for clueless descriptions

a good bar is a safe place to exhale
smiles the driver and later

sentences carried out anonymously
have a distinct air of cruelty

waking up to the news often relates to
everyone wanting something more than reachable

i agree in parts
soggy with rain

though no fault to the umbrella
strangers in flames is melting on a drenched napkin

promises are often broken
when seeking comfort

hinged in a dump truck
shadows chase shadows of themselves

drying the scribe readjusts blackouts into daydreams exercising
a state of mind vacation peeling from a billboard

shiny teeth rarely blow
continues the driver grinning

and your reflection improves
with my eyes closed

can you spot me a c note
i ask remembering

the last time he smiled this way
several pint glasses broke

the empty waste in your pocket
is a testimony to pot holes

look out the window sunshine
all roads crack and plastic cars rust

this does not help my situation living
underneath forgotten radars

often feels like time filling in
for an unhappy ending

how spared you have become
from explaining yourself clearly

what happens when self absorption
runs out of interest

you look like a bum dethroned
wearing that woollen hat he continues

in this migrating city
my mom made this hat i lie

listening to her say like hell i did
before cracking up yelling

now you go back down those stairs
i like living up here in the clouds

when the elevator stops elevating
i simply stay put

and lose count of the hours keeping me
from my favourite kind of day dreaming

beehive

dear doo little
doo do da day

sun beams through potted plants
and lands on once upon a time

they made up the hours performing
let us see what is out there

before the appearance of a shrieking cactus
disgraced the family flamingos thinking how beautiful

we were shuffling to the store
overly consumed with hummus

you felt relaxed enough to say
hard to believe life ends in perfection

*

instantly sealed cemetery idle
all i can spell today equates to

goofy goo
mysterious you

yet on the backs of scratch offs
some phantom proclaims

we reclaim the right to bail
with a bucket of holes bucko

inside a beehive
where a bulldozer of possibilities rages

louder than any vacuumed cave
littered with beads and those disposable crosses

like what they sell at
walmart

bead lady

gas lamps flicker with memories
ghosts mix with cures
and if we are lucky
a few forgotten remedies remain

i am convinced in time
creation made a few mistakes
and most agree in the dungeons of the vieux carre
the bead lady is one of them

through rusting cast iron railings
children crouch and laugh
before scampering from her necklaces
strung with shrunken plastic skulls
bus tickets and bones of fried chickens

dressed in a pink jump suit and a silver hard hat
i remember her predictions and prophecies
her claims to all who dared listen
how one day soon she would hide
from jehovahs endless gaze

and if you resembled a tourist
she would bow then hiss and spit
claiming your soul belonged to her
regardless of the departed

time pressed on through
and her prophecies left many out of breathe
in a world spilling over with misplaced keys

to this day
i see her dry clenched fists
offering obscenities knowing if the devil grew ears

he too would run from her drawling
threats to publically defecate

given my age
given what i have been given
how could i run from her
shrouded memory of persistence

how could I run understanding
her laughing wisdom
could change on a dime

and bless new orleans for protecting her
on bourbon street where unorganized crowds
wobble in meaningless fashion
where every honest prayer
can be answered with cash
in and out of strip joints and 24/7 bars

naturally we became friends
naturally i studied her craft
breaking oaths to drink into eternity

half baked years later
returning after the wreckage
her words follow the miles
beyond the cathedral steps
sickle in one hand a joke in the other
she was a one women carnival never to sell out
as caps and plastic cups adorn the streets

i am convinced i am cursed with her whispers
her touch and knowledge of dilapidated geography

sipping a double expresso
with a rind of lemon

with a belated family member
in the thick of the matter
in a casual sicilian run of the mill manner
i am given the scoop
and get fed the news
before stepping outside
noticing the sun burns blisters
on the loss of her shadow

happy cabbies take a smoke break

he wanted to be a sci fi writer unable to wake
refreshed in a floral painted room
the sun casts a new set of headlights
as happy cabbies
take a smoke break

sitting on the bus his senses fill
with images of sandy beaches and island girls
rocking in a bed of fresh curls
all the time knowing what he really can afford
lacks the funnies
as happy cabbies
take a smoke break

scouring 24/7 diners mumbling
prayers to the thin air
he asks forgiveness for the sharing
he has subjected everyone to

outside his apartment a neighbour
comments politely on how he seems to be
permanently sleepy and slightly stoned
just like those happy cabbies across the street
taking a smoke break

found objects

holding found objects up to the light
ripples in a leaf resemble a bottle broken

burned and freckled like a blue jay feather
or the lines in your hand taped together

invisible moving parts peel apart
trying to connect the dots

seeking something permanent
deeper than fragile helps find a way

to capture the wonder with a chance to return
into a world where we no longer

pluck out eyes to smell how to see
or stuff cotton wool in our ears to feel how to hear

the space between unlit streets
and burning trash cans that somehow bind us

back to being found objects
no longer afraid of the dark

brawling between two black eyes

there has been he slurred
there has been a leak in the mindless sieve

what are you talking about she screams
scowling at the stunted wanna be red head
squirming and shrieking on his lap

i mean exactly that he belches standing up
before slam dunking her emaciated body
against a full length mirror already cracked

a few rounds later a dressed sex guitar string
wrapped in a fuzzy corset
wiggles onto the greasy bar top

she is so drunk
the pole begins to bend

between two black eyes my lust is inspired
and wobbly proclaim chivalry is far from dead
knowing full well her punch nose
bombed out bouncer boyfriend dribbling
two tables over
wants to brawl for the right to stop her
disjointed bayonets bouncing in my face

i hand her twenty
itz on he shouts
unaware i have downed enough guinness
to nail this loser into the next frightful corner

for good this time

elvis is driving this crate

check out this cool gizmo
the driver grins fiddling a knob
after starting his car without a key

elvis is driving this crate
he beams adjusting the volume

i listen curled up in the front seat
trying not to think about the rest of my life

trying to forgive myself for leaving open
spaces somewhere deep inside

wild animal domestication it seems
has finally stampeded and broken loose
out of control and chasing fire

he will warn you when there is a cop ahead
or tell you when to speed or slow down

who will i ask distracted by the ants
eating out my insides

the king of course
who else he grins some more

studying the traffic passing i listen to the king warn us
when to avoid a left turn or make a necessary right

hazard up ahead baby
keep on going
business as usual

no please or thank you from elvis
no guilt addling his voice guiding me to the airport

finally outa here i try to smile
finally outa here destination unknown

with a soul running wild and a head filled with holes
thanks in part to elvis taking care of business

saints to go

he would be a saint
if he was born a catholic
a bayou mother manages to laugh
amidst the wreckage
and floating bottle tops
she once called home

with one cigarette on each busted lip
they work these saints to go
forty hour daze into extinction
wading knee deep
in cypress knees
with shopping carts
up and down sinking stairs
trying to extract and dry out
on a neighbours soggy porch
ninety five thousand ways to say
my stuff is no longer precious

hey slugger

hey slugger she said
how does it feel to lose a shoe
before you ever learned to tie the knot

does it remind you of our first encounter
with flesh folding flesh
in the back pocket of so many
well worn summers
with the sand and sun belching sedation
on the grit and dusty railroad tracks

do you mean on our thirsty something
in between bodies he replied
in a land you aptly named overflowing
with bloated gullets and pierced bellies competing
with sculpted torsos

when we worshiped bestial laziness
in the slowness of sucking on straws
splayed poolside writing postcards in the half lit
diffusion suspended in a looking glass hour

no she said
yr not even close
after all you were taking
lots of pills at the time

admit it we were two wrongs
determined to make it right
ignoring the bad breath mornings
forgiveness was never on the table

the fact is this
the torch at the end of the tunnel
had long been squelched in an ice bucket

before you insisted on trying to impress me
handing over twenty dollars in pennies
to an exhausted cashier for a couple of six packs
after we rolled like an unlucky coin back into town
dishevelled from speeding tickets and who knows what
and all you could say was can we do it again

hey slugger she said
whatever happened to your lists
and poems written on sidewalks
laced with squashed bollards
where you promised to hold me
wrapped in last breaths
before listening to the leaves
scratching across cracked concrete

hey he said you were the one who wrote
a car turns and the invader waits
with your hand in my pocket
and looking at you now with anticipation
barely able to prop me up
i bet you expect me to perform a side show
maybe help relieve your pain

not a chance she howled
slamming the door inches from his face
go home take a bath and call me
after you drown

crazy george

overhead clouds convulse
poverty breeds like mold

under the overpass
on a shutdown highway

crawling over broken glass
used condoms and gun clips

i often wish our creator could have taken
a little longer in creating

six days rarely cuts it after all
hell it seems is given a whole lot more attention

especially if you are unlucky or broken
or one more crazy george

it took him twelve torn minutes
while we searched for a working pay phone

as a vial of junk laced with bleach
burned through his brains

ghost rats

with bubble gum hair
they sit alone in huddled silence
on the cold concrete steps
outside closed gates of pristine
and freshly polished town halls

twitching and itching
some in need of a fix

perhaps hoping secretly inside
someone might notice them noticing
the lizard blank eyes barely blinking
as officials posture and grunt
waving yellow cards in the air
like flattened bananas unfit for chimps in a zoo

and given all the hoopla the press and reports
about drugs on the streets and property damage and abuse
given their age and the prospects given
grown tired of acceptance they spray the walls
before returning to rooms leaking with apathy
with the knowledge self worth often mirrors the society lived in
knowing they are lied to when we proclaim we care really
i mean really care what happens to our youth

partition extradition blame all we want and rant
condemn buildings yet to be built but the facts are clear
what we choose to ignore is left alone with a career
dish washing or cutting lawns in tax free castles

no more cash for our schools we bemoan and wail
the rising price of ice cream and yoga mats
has taken a toll on our health
and if we think they do not notice
alas i say a time will come

when they will be long gone
like ghost rats on a sinking ship
or more likely sleeping and weeping
wrecked in a morgue
someplace else much like this

labor day

words can never be
one dimensional

she smiles at the kitchen counter
opening a can of organic pinto beans

on the fridge smeared
with gmo free guacamole

worlds wither with travel
is written with magnetic letters

sounds like your poetry she says
with a mouth crunching tortilla chips

why is that he asks chopping
a flaking cluster of cilantro

because your poetry lacks
dirt between the ears

i thought you were all about
hygiene he squirms

except when it comes to the spoken word
wiping a lemon squeezer

before passing the salt
they sigh

blood brothers

the second time the knife pierced his chest
after the lights stopped buzzing
and long after a choir of angels sung

you have no power
except for a few broken and buckled
burnt out chords pumping
a lifetime of splinters

jesus wobbled onto the sliding street
resembling ice melting in a pitcher
laced with tequila

wiping the blood from his face he fumbled for a tip
to thank the bartender and undercover cop
for keeping him alive and far away
from his brother rafael

handcuffed and convulsing
on this bloody saw dust floor

3am feels smooth

3am feels smooth
cruising saint charles avenue

the unfolding cityscape collapses into collapsing angels
heaving anticipative breaths

a breeze ruffles our mops of wig hair
our minds funnel through the taxi windows
propped up by the humid hot air

the stench and fumes of existence
engulfs our nostrils and singes the senses
into a living giving molecule of refreshing life

rolling into happiness silver smiles screech past
as we try to name every smile
on every passing pedestrian face

patterns appear random and synchronized to sounds
life size vibrations bounce from our tongues
then float on past forever out of view

colliding cadences empty into unknowns
crying tears of ecstasy in the damp back seat of this
make believe chariot

thankfully our driver seems happy
for sure we are tipping him enough

yes 3am feels smooth
cruising saint charles avenue

although we cannot see any stars
we know they must be up there
commenting on how fast 25 miles per hour can feel

noticing how recognizable buildings
reconstruct themselves into ice cream monuments
as we laugh like ring tones before undressing
sending what is left of my mind
into delightful saturated confusion

and based on our purest wacky non being selves
i scribble on a parking ticket as our ride hits an open drain

you read my words then cry
then throw the ticket away

no damage done
we head downtown again

come all over my tingling teeth you laugh
wwoz is leaving the production line
with jazz burning with ecstatic soul
and rap beats pumping the dashboard

hypnotic across the windshield
the wipers swing commas and clown hats
with our feet dangling out the window
claiming everything tastes electric

you give the driver my last crumpled twenty
for sure our nerves are morphing
bouncing at the stoplight
diamond constellations replacing
the neon reds ambers and greens

passing underneath live oaks
wrapped in strange moss fabric
the meter is turned off
yet we keep on cruising

mister slow down you say
there are so many images we have yet to caress
so many humans on the tip of our tongues
at least until the night breaks free
at least until we stumble in a cloud of glitter
to find the curb has replaced this throne

tiptoeing into the audubon hotel
we wave thank you with a soft slew of see yall laters

dizzy with the unglued traffic
i watch our ride slide into the new day
noticing the remains of uncertainty have washed away the rain
in between the seconds and lifetimes mingling
with new beginnings and second chances
given freely perhaps as the universe parades
in its own unique way
to the vibes of new orleans

merry magdalene

like any good girl merry magdalene
ate all of her soapy lunch

now a sphere of flatulent gas explodes
into an ever increasing fungus state

one more lost fart in the world
she chuckles sitting next to a row of faceless eyes

believing her fading ego can compensate for talent
she recites dreams to imaginary crowds

cheering her on from the back of the bus
into an afterlife of carefree ease

without warning
brakes burn with rubber

this is the end of my wicker chair world
magdalene declares as the bus swerves into the curb

with her cane she starts rapping
on the heads of the confused passengers

wake up you sorry lot she shouts
this is our chance to throw it all away

no more walkers and diapers for me
yippee

magdalene put your seat belt back on
crackles the bus driver

and quit all that fidgeting and hollering
just remember before i call the day nurse

even great god almighty gets a flat
now and then

no matter what

no matter what blowing leaves
into the daze of a blinding day
carlos is consumed with a fire
knowing the cash in his back pocket
equates to decisions out of his control

clouds disperse
the hollow corners of yesterday
stuffed and stuck trying his luck
he shuffles clues from lawn to lawn
stained with lack of self expression
in search of positive exchanges
tossed into garbage bags
or recycled confession boxes

through a busy block he sways
to the prayers of others
as another minute slips thru
his cropped thatch of hair

how do you take it
the waitress asks alone
with bitten nails
as far as i can carlos replies
in broken english

both aware their options at best
remain limited

what is a town without a sound

what is a town
without a sound

a nameless place
without a face

a leafless garden
a hollow egg

cracked on
a silver spoon

jump on ripples
on a sea of song

dance on diamonds
inside and out

alive
in universal song

what is a town
without a sound

mama i am not scared
running through fire

to return home
in misty time

we can learn to rhyme
with word em up and superfly

what is a town
without a sound

a cage of homeless birds
yearning to fly

so sing in the sky

the grass is green
the sky is blue
this world
will never end

coffin maker

in a past life he made coffins for dead kids
recycled from cedar fencing

hand planed and carved
some found homes in museums

one fashioned into a coffee table
submerged in a luxury mansion

hewn relics
to hang out with other relics

a dozen were commissioned
by the house of blues

once a client asked for stained glass
to be inlaid with a cross

it should be noted however these coffins
did not stop the violence as intended

the dead keep getting stronger
as if training for some kind of gold medal

gutter punks

gutter punks
your name disturbs a capsulated youth
dumped on the lawns of pristine lifestyles
like an ever increasing bitter pill
we so want to shelve and refuse to swallow

gutter punks
your translucent eyes
swollen with hand grenades
have become a hit for the tourists

living examples of modern art run amuck
disposable garbage for someone else to bag
and silently ship off to unpronounceable wastelands
stinking of menthols and stale beer

gutter punks
pierced open with tattooed bellies
everyone fears your waves of purple hair
dangling in front of a cbs report
creating instant attention
until the next commercial break
sends us snoozing back to shop
or pose for a time delayed selfie

stare if you dare
look them square in blood shot eyes
see worn out tears on bearded baby faces

gutter punks
let us scrape together a little bus fare
burn down a state capital or two
singing give me a case of old english malt
and spare me some change

go dance until you fall in laughing heaps
repair ole glory with safety pins and hot glue

for you are every mayors
butt kicking nightmare

oh if wishes could come true
may you find a place somewhere sublime to play in
to make shadow puppets
and squiggly crayon masterpieces

maybe spray paint a new set of values
maybe print your own news
before going to bed with a warm glass of milk
safe from your hometown suburbia
where pet grooming clinics
outnumber health clinics
I betcha on average
thirty to one

clawing into a dream

katie wakes with images translating words
rejected from clawing her way back into
one too many day dreams

the first memory to scar her petal brow
resembles a cute baby smiling
until the pacifier came out

katie thinks her words rarely straddle
and often barely idle as if waiting
for a make believe dinner guest to arrive

turning her spaceship lamp on and off
with the precision of a technician
she has unlocked a process unavailable
in any textbook or online newsfeed

francine

francine recites the older i get
the more dead people i run into
and no matter how i try to distract myself
eventually the words find a blank sheet of paper
and for a brief time existence seems palatable

honey her mother frowns
you are only thirteen

oh mother it does not matter
you should have warned me
my therapist says we are all born
naturally unhappy

angst and melancholy are loyal friends
and no amount of searching for enlightenment
or studying the marquis de sade
can remove the pain of knowing
eventually i will have to grow up
unlike you

whispers lap his feet

whispers lap his feet
rainbow ribbons dart through water
resting beside a deserted shrimp boat
wave upon wave pile high then retreat
as the lost souls of past tides
ring through his ears

heat diffuses the sun
like a prisoner yearning to be released
scattering prisms dip then disappear
to a rhythm of fleeting seconds

his dry bones warm on the shoreline
passing children play with their gadgets
their footprints becoming passages
hidden in digitalized treasure

a lone pelican soars through his eyes
blinded for a moment on this gulf coast
feathers greet the flames
sailing through forgotten dreams

surrounded in the stench of another
man made disaster
he stops to inspect unturned shells
and the carcasses of rotting birds
nestled in the oil swept ridges

shaking his fist
the world of fools belongs to me
he writes with a stick

rain preacher

a troubled lord
sent me here
to save everyone of yalls
damned souls

i aint kiddin
or lickin
no fried chicken
no no no

i aint interested in
no saved souls
neither

because we all know
they know
where they are going

can you feel it
can you breathe it

are you ready to undress
and expose your ruin

can you feel it
can you breathe it

i aint interested in
no small talk
neither

i aint kiddin
nor repeatin
or lickin no

damn fried chicken
not when it boils down
to yr lost soul

no
no
no

pay back

years later so elegantly you wrote
i have swallowed you in gratitude and for rent
you swallowed me whole and collect
yet now without warning these porous walls
no longer await intrusion to drool over nonsense

just give me back something sometime
remember you ended with no thanks
before slamming the door
confirming the facts
as long as we both do as you say
for the rest of our borrowed long lost daze
time will pass relatively smoothly

cash flow

when little else to do
caught him red handed
chilling in a holding cell
t ball later told me
cash flow goes
something like this

when i need me some money
it magically appears
all i have to do
is follow a few golden rules

first things first

i carefully wipe clean
my ole shuggie otis
and make sure the barrel
shines like a diamond

then i let the caps mingle
in ma silver skull ashtray

when i think i have done a good job
i stop thinking
and do it all over again

the first time when i am shining
i make sure not to remember
a damn thing

the second time i focus on the ass
going to get squeezed
as soon as the job is done

helicopters

*

this fleeting moment always steamy half suspended
yes she says sipping a warm beer with a straw
we were always fighting and yelling obvious extremes
but did he have to go out last night and lose
continue with your statement for the record please
helicopters are flooding out the stars the sky
before five bullets claimed a murder
living beside this hospital felt somewhat comforting
daze seem to have over extended themselves since
almost out of sight and never within reach
mangled into digital lives and slogans
into worth and notice
before five bullets claimed a murder
on the porch their propellers often made our hair curl
their mechanical whirring sent invisible signals
without the radio bleeping cosmic smiles
kinda like how i sleep now
propped up against a flat tire
once their safe landing equaled a place
to rest and reassess the measurements of success
before five angry bullets
claimed a state capitol murder
what we take for granted often almost feels sacred
living large on the bayous trenched deep in the one six

*

after the parade and funeral salutations
after a thousand uniformed bikes have been well polished and fed
this magnolia seems to be the last one weeping
this crepe myrtle blossom perhaps a delicate gift of blood

*

i admit without measure or judgement
for the past month i am tubing between rebel flags and daiquiris

chemical plants and okra
this state of being follows me wherever i go
into the shadows where live oaks bow
fifteen hundred miles can seem like a ways
or a long shot before a safe exit
before my toes and fingers are dipping
for another dance on bayou ridge road

*

so what about today and care of a future
so what about the folks volunteering without pay
so what about the displaced the fractured and unforgiving
the shirtless mothers swaddled in debt
so what about the thousands forced living in shelters
or worse finally realizing hope is for suckers
so what about the guy trying to get back on his feet
and the countless businesses gone flat broke on a joke
so what about the priest who cares for his parish
and the cop on the beat who believes in helping a child
so what about neighbour and his three barking dogs
and the stray cat pissing along the fence
so what about this flood water riddled with scum
belching out toxins we use to colour our hair
so what about the farmers losing their crops
or my mother who just wants to sip coffee and write
so what about this state you claim only fools can live in
or worse is spawned by racist bigots
so what if it continues to rain for another week or so
this news can never sell a shiny bmw
so what is going to happen feels beyond our control
the great usa won another olympic gold medal

skew whiff sockets jam na na beats

skew whiff sockets jam na na beats
and according to dali everything is cannibalistic

t fly agrees because today is mardi gras
in this floating hotel fried from the inside
where shotgun rooms lust for beaded symbols
manufactured in sweat shop hells

*

loaded parties dress up before scurrying as roaches
to squeeze the dream into broken bathrooms
for a daily dose of claustrophobic celebration
driven in frustration for an ongoing climax
knowing this might be all there is to own

a simple slice maybe of one more
once in a lifetime moment
for the split and sniff smokers
and the gooey glued gosh guys
the be alls and the end alls
the beings of no colour

arriving as one open mouthed bubble
clutching glistening glasses that chink then smash
into slices of happiness and forgotten offerings
for the next confession box or hysterical depression

*

no one cares about the mess
except for a few born again slaves
chasing up and down bourbon street
until the moron carrying a life size wooden cross
breaks down for a beer with a transgender nun
who is digesting acid with a band of ravers

mingling with plastic daises and a recently laid angel
weeping her way through erotic bliss

*

breathless again
in a strange kitchen come diner
cum borrowed womb
surrounded by sacrificial smiles flashing
purple and gold teeth
my skin feels reality itching
as unthinkable tribes reappear to arrange
folded up chairs and ladders on wheels
propped up for the best view

have you not heard
king zulu is in town

*

a goddess hands me a coconut
before the thrown away treasure
disappears into the jigsaw crowd

swaying in vain with hands joining legs
a dali painting emerges
constructing a soft landscape
with hard boiled beans and plastic beads

*

not a thing left to shoot up here
someone yells with a twang
stepping over as we cry in and out of happiness
after kissing a coconut with a mouth
filled with a hot dog who moments later
devours us with added mustard

chaucer

in older well trodden parts of london town
conversations often end with fists and broken glass
honestly we were too pissed most of the time to remember
the more memorable ones forgotten
for better or worse the other day
i found myself privy to something like this

yo how come you havent
havent what
fucked her yet
yr no raging stud
try red bull and vodka
sure he aint fucked her
look at those tits
fuck all that just ask her
ask her what
she is standing over there
go on i dare you
get the fuck out of here
before my old man
gives you a fucking hiding
core blimey who pissed her off
lemme see fuck me
you been hiding a full pack of smokes
bad to be smoking anyway
says who you my fucking doctor now
are you going to fuck her or what
fuck you she has lost her marbles if she does
let me remind you mate you are not fucking her marbles
look a burning butt just fell into her glass
smouldering images create a gothic effect
who cares are we fucking off or not
i feel like a kebab
yr too fucked up to drive
says who fuck face

bartender give him a red bull
and fucking vodka for the road
why so he can go fuck with her marbles
fuck off the lot of yer
i am getting a taxi
what about her
she can walk i am starving to death

mona always knew

from the get go mona always knew
how to remind us of a time
when your new tv flew out
the third floor dorm window
before abstract guilt sent us flying
down flights of slippery stairs

you sulked about campus
ignoring the debaters
until mona bust down the door
wedged the tv on your head
and turned the fucker back on

living in desperate times
is no longer an excuse mona wailed
and to prove her point we rehearsed
the apocalypse helicopter sequence
underwater with plastic violins
three times a week

now years reassemble themselves
into a long time later
after surviving so many bloody wars
mona reads a screeching streetcar
her fingers have mutated into
stained porcelain cigarette holders

i am letting yall know she slurs
a slow death like mine
will make you thirst for a life
not worth pissing away
in this waxed dixie cup

almost alone

in the closeness of rain
touching rain
soft rhythms comfort
an inner desire to remain
flowing with the movement
from puddle to stream
and back again

a few hours prior
she clearly remembers how
they wrestled to become one
cleansed in smiles with mud
congealing between their toes

are we slipping or sinking
she says watching him stumble
towards the shadows
to stoke a fire
before crawling back
into the flames

knocked out with a head cold

after the endless party
a bloody birthmark stains the sheets

senseless mingles with cocaine
mingles with a mother and her regret

his knife is washed clean
knocked out with a head cold

watching as you ponder what to wear
both fully aware another life has gone off

someplace else
to sleep

this plague we consume has learnt well
and taken advantage of the tick and the flea

the mosquito and the rat sucking on themselves
before spitting out what is left only to deal with cops

ceremonially placed on a mirror
a daily ritual reflecting lost hours

today resembles many a yesterday
you choose a cotton skirt laced with forget me knots

both know what it feels like to be famished
with cold pop eyes on the table

stepping downstairs seems to be far enough
for the chosen broken few if you really want to know

fidgeting behind dark glass tears
routines bend over backwards

until once the service is over
they shuffle back up three flights of filthy stairs

reunited with a life searching for
someplace else to weep

dizzy echoes of tomorrow

dizzy echoes of tomorrow

the
clanking
cranking steel
hurls him thru time
zones sitting in a one horse
carriage with thoughts and reminders
staring out the windows identifying
with a trembling icy landscape
beaten again inside the
dizzy echoes of
tomorrow

his
guts are
grappling
for a will to eat
a dried up sesame
bagel and the coffee stain
on his jeans resembles a land
he recently escaped from
his soul aches with
a splinter or two
found in the
tears of her
eyes

he
sits here
as an old man
privileged in his dreams
reflects on an age of waste
where clocks and systems fail to
communicate the love he has breathed
and released into recycled actions
passed down from countless

fights where chaos
plagues each new
gift and every
worn out
prayer

he
spies
on the
platform
an unlucky sparrow
crunching a tick
held in its
broken
beak

the
grace of
rusting cans
helps divide his stardust
gaze inward like a pack of razors
wants to bleed this
poem dry

a
girl
sitting
next to him
is talking on
her phone about
selfies made in a mirror
with her sweat
mingling
with
his

she

reminds
him of a time
he took a hit of acid
and walked through walls
long before the matrix
made the stuff legal
and does all
he can to
ignore
her

he
asks
melting
in a reflection
if the idea to
rhyme is
a dying
art

trying
to sleep
closed curtains
beg to be opened
dried up oil paint on his
hands are cracking into a premonition
while an abandoned hangover lingers in his veins
what is left of the shine on his boots starts to
reflect the miles travelled to feel grateful
before he dismisses the need to unload
a text message for your eyes only
knowing it is merely a cheap
exercise to compensate
for a petty crime
of passion

inside a william coleridge dream

bound in a world unhinged
inside a william coleridge dream

floating underneath willow trees
dancing in your hair alongside sights unseen

slivers of gold disguised as leaves
touch our bodies and comfort bare feet

laced with wonder erased from care
the final temptation of forgiving lost time

believes breath is a gift
delicately inked onto skin

*

bound in a world
with a final last chance
held deep within
like a drop of water

waiting to be released
from a rusting tap
dripping in a sink filled
with broken dishes

message received

message received and understood
forget the facts simply leave an impression

somewhere in between
casual and smart

a french cuffed shirt perhaps
missing a cufflink

or my old mans shiny paisley tie
thumb creased over the years

and worn in all his holy places
even now as he rests here cold as stone

expecting me to find the guts
to dig a hole and bury him

avocados sound like hand grenades

huddled on a stoop sipping leftovers
reflected in a rain tinted street
a pink dawn appears harmless enough

we have been up all night
and i am poised to lay on my charm
if she will ever stop talking that is
about the beauty of moths trapped in puddles
and the inevitable on coming ice age

across the street motions become hums
a pack of frustrated clowns jog past out of breath
before an old man appears wearing untied shoes

that would be lizard she says lighting a cigarette
he acts out sometimes but for the most part
he is a harmless sort

does he ever move
from the middle of the street
i ask pretending to care

she ignores my question and continues
he has the weirdest eyes
whiter than any moon
they make me so sad and remind me of the time
i lived with an avocado tree in the backyard

you have lost all of me now
i say knowing nothing is going to happen today
or for that matter any time soon

when the avocados fell onto the tin roof
they sounded like hand grenades
going off in my head

i see i say standing up and shoving off
noticing the old man with the sad moon eyes
remains standing perfectly still
in the middle of the street
staring at his untied shoes

downtown houston

pink clouds pollute
this sunday morning

silent pristine buildings
are locked down tight
except for a slew of fast food joints
and chock a block churches

the stench downtown clearly states
this is the wrong place to try and cool off
for anyone missing shoes

a car passes with chrome exhausts
drumming metallic beats

a window rolls down then a bottle hits him
hard on his knee

the missile shatters
and his bare feet step through glass

like a shadow seeking shelter
be hobbles underneath the overpass

shouting to the passing car at least you noticed me
at least someone has seen

before folding back into a cardboard box
to sleep away the unforgiving day

dagger dodge and his sharpie logic

sipping shitty beer with ice
in a plastic cup through a straw
mimicking cats claw
his legs wrap around
a bandaged bar stool

no one is talking
because no conversation
is deemed necessary
in this meditative intermission
nailed to leaking floors
was it sixty hours or sixty years ago

thru swinging peeling doors
the urinal pipes are broken beside his feet
a ring on his finger reflects from a pool
what he once added on these peeling
graffiti stained walls

the rules of love
are never known

last seen wearing the rags of his own undoing

hiding in the corridors of yesterday
wearing the rags of his own undoing
in a state of bubbles with glass diamonds bouncing
an image of starvation makes it impossible
to ever want to cross the road

all this talk about saving an abandoned school
has left him unable to forgive
the persuasion of voting

meanwhile all around him
schools where real children
huddle in learning
flake in decay

a shadow grips false teeth
hollow reincarnations speed past
a plastic bag lays gently at his feet

coffee made him a zombie
yet again quitting is trying
to conquer his soul

breaking in and walking through this
abandoned once cherished school

he feels like a stranger
capable of missing an odd shoe

on the blackboard someone scrawled
friendship can be a pain
that never seems to go away

stumbling forward up and down stairs
past benches and desks
stacked like a burton clock tower

on a notepad he stitches
clarity whispers

back on the street
organic sun lotion
replaces a december snow

this yule night is not so much
about being sucked into commerce
more like how can we recognize
each other as faceless facts
and the ever growing baggage in their eyes
makes forgotten luggage and tongues
lick contaminated wounds
with the common complaint
barking more parking
parking
parking

too much is never enough
and for a place all about nature
where are the footpaths and bicycles

*

close by
a bartender follows him with razor glares
between his ears he cries in the sawdust room
ver messe ver messe
who is going to clean up this bloody mess

back home a flashlight passes over
a few twigs creak

undisturbed
he stitches some more

written down words
often require written down violence

as a dead school lives on
the living school dies

sometimes the more civilized we are
the more we forget civilization

in passing

beside a shallow edge
on a cool marble path

forgotten monuments
lives gone by

lead towards
a hand carved stone

hidden in weeds
aching for sound

he stoops and weaves
like a falling leaf

and reads beneath
this grave

lie thoughts
from you

letters written

these blocks of wood
thrown onto the fire
were once another mans craft

carefully planed
then shaped and sanded
i have spilt force with an axe

slicing this work
into convenient pieces
now stacked obscure and waiting

paint screws and all
to be char disfigured
paper weight remains

nurse bertie

apples are dropping early this year
meanwhile high noon on magazine street
corner kids with masks
play on the buckled roots of live oak trees

standing in the middle
between the celebrations
nurse bertie is on her way to work

late last night she got a phone call
from the other side of this half raised town
her youngest great grandchild
doa the cop politely said

now she studies the cracks in pavement slabs
her body shaking in polished shoes
and a freshly starched pressed uniform

determined not to cry
or make a fuss
until christmas rolls around

blood sports

freezing tears roll down her cheeks
melting as they fade an image of youth

leaving a damp mark on the neck of his sweater
worn in style for the very last time

as she lets the ice in
as she leads herself out

wrapped in a baggy suede coat
a reminder of flesh he is unable to skin

see how she sleeps

see how she sleeps
on mistletoe leaves

white on white freckles
droplets of curls

all in slow motion
recalling a passion

rising from threads
sown out of fear

i have used these lines before
but cannot remember the sensation

there is an itchy caterpillar hidden
in these rhombus pants

old man darwin

hats off to old man darwin
drawn in bibliopolic proportions with relapses roaring
he managed to crawl out from the primordial ooze
wrapped in a shell of his own creation

searching for hidden clues to rewrite
unreadable textbooks
and define where we came from
without any god given explanation

yes he figured it out
did old man darwin
where we need to go
and where we are now

ignoring frowned perspectives or perspiring fools
believing adam and his apple was plucked from a tree
by the reptilian hands of a ravenous whore

regardless of nose hair his mind meshed with time
and came back intact

and what he thought might once be habitable
and a source of new beginnings
alas becomes another lost tourist trap
in a dead end continent
where business remains cut throat
in a world where born again fires
continually rage
and busted payphones
haunt me

shiny white teeth

oh to be so happy
with a fresh set of shiny white teeth
oh to know
i can never be cured
oh to be so happy
with my shiny white teeth
oh to know
i only devour
oh to be so happy
with shiny white teeth
before an uzi goes off
with a whoops and a sigh
oh to know why
a million trillion fake dollars
swims in blood
congealing at our feet

following the footsteps of ghosts

a broken umbrella sails through the air
past bloated pigeons and a banksy sighting

overlooking the river edge
scenes collide with broken glass

ripples recede leaning on a rusting balcony
peeling paint sticks to bloody bare feet

inspecting a forgotten splinter
i watch a stranger watching me

as sirens replace whispers
and shadows stain the rain

another battle for a castaway island
has again reclaimed so many birthmarks

forced now to borrow clean shirts and shovels
to dig fresh graves for wandering friends

albeit smashed with so it goes
i accept no amount of cures can save them

with endless directions
following the footsteps of ghosts

the slog of ink

all it can take is an image falling
across a reflection ready to burst
when the heart beats open again

*

fluttering moth wings above bottles of wine
now emptied and holding candles with flame
cast shadows across the corners of this borrowed womb
before becoming waves trapped in the moonlight
with a slim chance of healing a scar or two
across his busted face
across his bare bone skin

*

hands touch the rain bursting
from cascading stars
before stepping back inside
to dance with the paint caught in a net
filled with abandonment
under a spell yet secretly knowing
his art is useless unless you appear
across the blank page
beyond the random arms
and polite conversation
making the slog of ink
recognizable again

on this feisty carnival parade

on this feisty carnival parade
where furry caterpillars crawl and munch
on purple and gold mashed potato beads
beneath tippy toe expectations
reminders keep on thinking
i might break my neck out here
scavenging plastic in vanities hope
to sail on uncharted seas
knowing fate often deals
too many displaced jokers

hunter

punching the keys
he wakes to the sounds of his last victims scream

his starch collar fibres unravel at the seams
as dribbles of sweat stain a gonzo shirt

the painted slogans he never believed in
seem to coil around one too many parched throats

yesterday no matter how far away he witnessed
two silver shadows dance in the doorway

past the caviar and champagne sips
laced with flippant success

a knife slid into the last exit out of here
unable to panic the door lock broke

and bullets riddled through
his barrel paisley chest

nothing as usual was reported
and a few weeks later beside an unmarked grave

crows scavenged the dirt
and suited men dressed like the crows

stood guard with the statue
lingering in the mist

secure in the knowledge
a new set of slogans were already in play

under the shade of any old moon

childhood memories bloat with confusion
combing back loose hair
one minute i am a sabre tooth tiger
ripping bed sheets laced with ginseng
the next clutching straws muddled in thin air
avoiding passing head lights
beaming over shrinking ceilings

this has to be an elaborate trap
every year before santa arrives
with unanswerable questions
crammed with chocolate
rifled from a woollen sack

today if i ask what if
all i get is some guy upstairs
always remember your feelings
are never really the facts

i hate facts i wail
i want feelings again
the numb dumb ones gift wrapping gifts
have to be better than none at all

i know we held them once
lip to lip and word on word
smoking shared cigarettes
under the shade of any old moon

now it appears between hot cider and eggnog
i am a scaled fish ready for the fryer
lost inside a nightmare
perfected by my own way of thinking
a learning curve spiralling off the charts
swimming in shadows of rancid oil

counting words carefully watching you
refold tissue paper with the ability to fend off
diluted conversations
one click away from i am okay
to thank you very much for asking

this age ignites candle lit numbness
and in the corridors before we died
i miss the battles and quit your bitchin
go sulk with your clash was always a favourite

i miss the report back after taking your meds
and the order to look out the window
before go jump out the window
go feed the cat try reading a book
do anything except pace saying it is a job

yes lie if you have to
go on try it for size
before dreams shatter the half filled glass
with a mouth stuffed with carrot cake
quitting sugar is easy
living in a land laced with ultimatums
score charts mark his and hers
where is my hat
here is your halo

slamming the door
my face feels the ice
bouncing along the floor
i am done you say
maybe i will call you later
but if there is a reply
if there is a text or hint of a ring tone
i do not like i am going to reply
very calmly at first

you can cook the flowers tonight honey
i am out reliving your poetry

which one i ask can i text back
the shitty one pause of course
some say they are all shitty
i text back
no this is one of your classic
wanna be romantic shitty ones

can you tell me how it all ends
something about sharing cigarettes
under the shade of any old moon

vaccine city

vaccine city
with your closed gates and homeless limbs
blocked up arteries discharging chemical masterpieces
another lost hole nowhere close to becoming found or round
yet somehow fitting snugly into a quarter pounder
with plastic cheese and rubbermaid pickles
the size of another spent spat out god

vaccine city
a stone throw away before touch down
mixed sensations drown out expectations
boxes of hairspray and fresh nylons
unload limping illusions past gnawing guards
convincing us we must stay awake
on these streets once paved in gold

vaccine city
close up hack breath highlights
tinge in brackish sunshine
and far below the burger king moon
a crack beggar fights a white levi junkie
on their knees they are learning
to crawl crying with bloody eyes closed
both needing more fresh lines to save them from
how come this never ever stops happening
or goes anything like close to my way

alas vaccine city has sprung a leak
and evaporated into a melting pot
humanity might well piss away
just ask the wilted cocks and robbers
who forget to close their mouths when consuming
how comfortable others have become
numbed in self explanations and borrowed footnotes
plotting revolutions to fit faux designer knock offs

bubbling in a maze of wasted withdrawals
and what to quit next before we all wake up
as old men strung out on chit chat
filled to the brim knowing
what if is never a real question
when considering the toxic canisters
two doors down the hall
have sprung a leak

vaccine city
at least admit everyone is stoned
and completely paranoid
and can barely find the haystack
let alone another clean needle
perhaps a bleeding excuse might/maybe
change our collapsed minds
relapsing into a self rejected state
where boredom is the new dysfunctional
keeping everything in place
because our children know
speaking never made language
as easy as texting
after watching their parents
fumble with words they can never ever
permanently delete

vaccine city
these shivering streets
are backed up into turf war corners
with zone missions and take outs
and a handful of honest lads swearing
we will never be ready for real this time
to take bill burroughs seriously

vaccine city
passing out jack boots and tar skinned jackets
to anyone capable of throwing a punch

while an overdressed hippie type
shoots up a ghetto catholic
before zig hailing into the bank
asking for body parts to feed
a gang of misplaced zombies

vaccine city
once known for her views
sits alone now in a constant overdraft
huddled in pockets of cataracts
long gone off the media charts
semi submerged to become
the perfect isolated nightmare
forever waiting in the wings
with one or two lonely cough phlegm hackers
wearing stylized shades and holding up painted signs
honk
if you want to get out of this war

can we honestly believe humanity has trampled on
their cardboard castles
before retreating into bunker thick concrete
three miles under
to regroup and lick open wounds
feeling a sense of completion
and another mission accomplished

vaccine city
beyond surreal
swaggering in closed circuits and misguided catv cables
after the cops quit protecting selective parts
and who can blame them in this suffocating fog
where his/her collective stare is no longer concerned
with table manners as loathsome bionics
mingle with federal prosecutors
busted for lining their own fat pockets
to feed ever thirsty for profit prisons

their defence claiming anything goes
as long as we keep the amex churning
spewing out bills onto spewed on streets
who cares about clean water
when we can manufacture it wholesale

vaccine city
on every street corner
four way cameras have become
an overpriced response plugging up real time
calculated by assigned blunt scissor hands
ready to cut out faint beating hearts
before the next great fry up begins
with a molotov cocktail
thrown towards a slashed poster
flapping on a boarded up class room door
leaving a blood stained message
for the next teacher to scrub clean
and the constant reminder
for every child to read
however true or false
as seen on tv
with a fake badge and a gun
i can be anyone

savannah

savannah tapes together her shaking fist
into a voice filled with sea shells and curls
before a salt shaker explodes
sprinkling good fortune all over
her lucky customers

savannah drops bacardi bottle in the middle of the night
then giggles as the shattered glass sparkles on the floor
the broken shards i remember well
matched the stars in her fireside eyes

i worshipped your lips
your closing hours and weekend benders
your flowing hair of forest coal
and eyes filled with secrets like oyster pearls
the songs you sang skipped and tattooed my skin
as our bodies rolled up air tight through the night
hiding out for days with buster keaton tapes
performing on ourselves his black and white stunts

why did i agree
we should never spell out our names
beneath sagging branches of a magnolia tree
dripping with stinging caterpillars
i was a disused salesman fresh out of pain
then and sometimes now
you an intricate clock
sensually over wound
a sweet pea liquorice stick
i could not stop licking

savannah remember when you wrote
we should pretend love never exists
as a streetcar swiped a crow feeding on the tracks
later that night pinning me to the floorboards

ceiling and walls
we rolled through a kama sutra canon
until you realized my clip art was peeling
and life was determined to dribble on down
placing its unwanted self on the shelf marked goodbye
sending us back packing into our own separate tombs
to rename the scars
separate and daydreaming

myth

the daze of morning stumbles on
the remains of an opened beer

fingers find a pair of lace up boots
a mosquito anticipates the next move

neither seem to care who wins or loses
who is bitten or finally squashed

breathe

not to clear the air but fill the air
with songs and smiles
desire and dreams

not to clean the air but dirty the air
with sweat falling
from rain soaked limbs

lick it dry
kiss it smooth
jab it hard
kick it in

feel it enter
let it go
through fingers
through tears

dive within
enjoying what is left

just in case
it all goes

as long as i pay the antitheist today

oh pale and fleeting laughing
where faces are washed
in what is left behind
in the silt stained mud of tomorrow
pressing memories against a mirrored glass
blocked by idle domesticated views
and endless cavities
stuffed and squeaking
with forked tongues

leave me here
to zip up these eyes
walking through a town
where crack in the alley teaches fools
to ignore kangaroo wars
and prove again and again
the self righteous answer prayer
albeit with torture

*

for what can be worse
than a past persistently caught up
in keeping down the future
except perhaps an ever present past
going ahead of the future

numbing into acceptance
countless classroom murders
obesity and our obsession
to pollute great rivers and streams
leaving me to ask how and what the fuck when
did logical thinking become imprisoned in dogmas
until along faux marble corridors
lined up in stone cold waiting rooms
filled with the lost and beguiled and damned

the price for health depends on
forgetting in sickness
all breath is the same

burnt out star

filled with frozen splinters
you turn on the gas in our make believe balloon

the stars are burning out tonight
you wave climbing onto the slippery roof

undecided i follow
like a wet blanket needing warmth

noticing a constellation
dangles in a galaxy of claws

towards the milky way
our shared breath smokes

with a chance to forget
how remote we behave

on the ground
four flights below

unnoticed shadows cast
speckled patterns and squares

passing pedestrians
laced with snow

make you ask is it safe to say
before we freeze

will these flames inside
restore the belief

if we stay entwined
common sense will flee

and we can sleep as one
forever

clear skies and chap stick

crashing into a blanket of bracken
after hours driving

too fast past signs
reeking of obstacles

freshly steam rolled tarmac
obscure hedge like trimmers

senses are displaced against the dashboard
refracting puddles of broken glass

you are so vain you once said
i bet you would check your hair

in the rear view mirror
before exiting an exploding car

stumbling through storm drenched fields
i guess she was right again

thinking of what has yet to happen
on the couch behind the shower curtain

caught in the madness of texting and driving
too nervous to hang up

creates delusions however fleeting
to someday wrap night jasmine around her hair

and disconnect the reality
limping down this hill

six hundred miles
from where you are now

spinning with the ways of the sun

spinning
with the ways of the sun

revolving around
on a daily basis

in the heat and humidity
of starlit barrooms

in much the same way
as a stack of hot bills

silently sits
on this kitchen table

*

spinning
with the ways of the sun

yes we are happy
like the stack of hot bills

sitting right here
on a kitchen table

with the ways of the sun
revolving around

on a daily basis

*

fossil onlooker

fossil onlooker
i come here honestly
knowing we have done this all before

in muddy catfish pools crawl a little deeper
until i am part of this dish detergent scape
until i am connected

fossil onlooker
being one with the peeling bark of dissected trees
i seek the truth of ticks to elevate a voice
reflecting across a land i once called home

shielding the undergrowth
i find a skull complete and safe
from the raw sewage spewing overhead

the idea of living inside a brittle intricate structure
sends me running to follow fresh tracks
laced in the oily choked mud knowing
on these river banks a new moon ago
we were faceless bystanders
filthy in the wreckage
never imagining one day possibly today
all the commerce and energy spent in making us perfect
could end up as toxic waste

fossil onlooker
abstract thought needs no footing or foliage
no future or myth to reveal tar feathered truth
clogging our veins as children google
how to implant tits the size of tombstones
and what seems to some the new be all and end all
is breaking out into a rash

and what is now called radical
at best is spray painted by banksy
into slogans to cut up and post abandoned
and discarded in puddles reflecting my own denial

odours haunt me

on the platform
in the middle of london bridge station
with pigeons and commuters
following the routines
regulated by daily living

everyone appears busy
and seemingly unconnected

sipping coffee served up
in snack bars and cafeterias
with weird girly names
i will say this once
odours haunt me

watching packaged sandwich wrappers
float past the sounds of work boots
and oxycontin junkies
begging for loose change
i accept standing where i have stood before
allows me to report
england is far from dying

merely digging her heels in
a little deeper than usual

christmas tree

this product requires assembly
however no tools are necessary

the instructions are inside the carton
important notice

this merchandise was inspected
and delivered to the carrier

in perfect
condition

it has been specially packaged
to withstand ordinary handling

batteries are not included

squeeze the dream

draw nearer into the light
not so shy anymore

singe wings over marooned miles
lost and gained

laugh and burn listening to the news
battle on buckled rotten bed frames

let us bury ourselves deeper in the abstract belief
these slipping moments can last forever

if we squeeze the dream out of our veins
and lick open wounds clean to the bone

mickey mouse is weeping

mickey mouse is weeping
there seems so much left to do
when tolerance becomes a past tense
compassion a four letter word

mickey mouse is weeping
news reports minnie has gone and overdosed
on one too many prescription pain pills

hosing splayed guts off a disco ball
bloody reflections mingle with soggy glitter
across a mirrored dance floor

mickey mouse is weeping
thankfully on bourbon street again

tears are washing grown men
grind on sweating men
as strong backed women tongue
warm wet cunts

*

mickey mouse is weeping
a ranking senator is preaching
his voters pray for sudden death
to strike a nigga president

*

massacred on a twittered landscape
no change from the white washed capitol

no half mast rainbow flags
no god blessing to end this hate

mickey mouse is weeping
in gettysburg climbing cemetery hill

history shivers
as i embrace the rebel yell
yes mickey mouse is weeping
and i am no wiser than before

a loaded rifle sits beside a child
sleeping in my arms

in the crystal night of knowing

a ferryman casts off from a burning pier
sounds of waves crash against rocks

echoes from worn ropes of fluttering flags
predict a storm warning approaching

wet paint on their hands
cancel unknown questions

he notices her boots have a new set of laces
and claims he is mad enough to dive into icy water

and feel the sea gulls laughter
ricochet over plastic balloons

far out past the sun
night explodes

beside the lapping edge a voice reflects
once we were one

submerged with sea horses
galloping before us

in the crystal night of knowing
shards of glass reflected choirs of stars

following our fingers
no longer sweating

when clawing out of sand and silt
digging deeper the surface breaks into splinters

and explodes into a mystery
to scratch on the walls who else is there

as pelicans glide overhead
close enough to hear their wing beats

close enough to witness eternity flash by
in a blink of their wounded eyes

two pressure cookers

the kettle boils steam
ejecting a whistle

i want to scream
about my ole mate patrick

and his two pressure cookers
squealing in our tight kitchen

gotta sterilize
ma needles he purred 24/7

melting on acid to ink in
savage lasting beauty

zapatista

painted words on peeling paint
blister as rust blooms beneath the sweat

red stained eyes of knowledge unite in burnt smiles
as workers plough into thoughts

aqua spills above the shackles
souls within etch out a chant

nació
la palabra en la sangre

screaming language deafens language screaming
as rivers of progress run up the town hall steps

sacred bones already edible
collect on the walls of prison hell cells

and no matter how many times
the sentence is faked

and no matter how many times
the noose is lowered

power survives in their woven faces
and grows with the corn towards the light

the word the word
is written in blood

going up in flames

time to gather up the clowns
and dispose of red noses

pack a tent if it helps
go look for a fresh glass to drown in

i admit i prefer streets
to cow fields

and take strangers laughing pissed
over freshly picked flowers

always day dreaming
the clouds rolled in

my favorite part of the calendar
your felt tipped xxx

giving the rise in crime
it is reassuring to know

before i run out of smokes
the flames in your eyes

might save us both
tonight

jarret

it is all about
that time again
because history
says why notice
the displaced
have yet to return
to their broken
misspelt homes

it is all about
this time again
to wash off the walls
post hurricane vomit
and take a long hard stare
at our no man lands
dividing us from them

it is all about
through sickly sips
of organic tea
and marmalade toast
to notice the glittering
metallic cadillac swerving
through unlit streets

because history
says so what
with the big white
n word booming
into the big black
n word school zone

or not
just because
history says so

mister keys

insipid knots dangle and scratch his brow
fake austerity combs thru thinning hair

nicotine stained nails claw on imaginary ladybugs
as he inspects a postcard taped to a kitchen wall

yesterday he built polling booths
and the week before that a pinball machine

dressed now in a blank sheet
he locks himself up for freshness sake

quarrelling over yogurt mold
and debts incurred at greyhound stations

will she

will she be as mysterious as an egg
wear earrings to bed
let me wipe the salt from her lips
igniting the fires within our eyes
to follow this coastal path
above a stain stormed sky
looking for a place
where poets collide

will she laugh as we collapse
into the ferns under the covers
before resting on my chest
between each breath
raging in a storm
searching for a place
where poets collide

will her hand fold into mine
into a space yet to be defined
safe from the prattle of commerce
and deafening ring tones
plagued with commitment
and half baked promises
as we melt on the steps
where hungry waves meet
quivering like feathers
above the clock tower
searching for a place
where poets collide

will her smile open the moon
entwined in an embrace
as i take her hand
with her heart on my lap
listening to the ocean

whisper this is the place
floating in space
adrift in song
where poets collide

what falls thru the night

what is lost in the night
can be found in the morning

a bouquet of dead flowers
dented cans and plastic furniture

all swept ashore
emerging as afterthoughts

where tides reveal time
flowing swiftly backwards

*

footprints retreat
yet appear closer

as a blanket of fire
drips into daylight

as a heron soars through
heaven bound eyes

*

what falls through the night
can be discovered in morning

in the wing beating wind
there you are again

sparkling limbs
swimming with remembrances

far out at sea
whispering to me

can you feel the salty air
healing open wounds

do you see
do you see

the lost sons and daughters
hands raising through the surface

signaling then falling as the endless blue
swallows their warning

*

what falls through the night
can be found in the morning

she ushers closer
as he enters water

a shooting star wish
whispers might wake them

without reason

wanting to move
closer to reason

climbing into
an abandoned building

shadows stain the walls
in the sticky lead dust air

corridors and closets
become a maze

mimicking my mind
as i pause at a note

carefully taped
to a rusting locker door

some reassembled memento
some clip art of lost time

drops to the floor
without any chance to forgive

pills of questions
cursing through veins

beware the toes you step on today

beware the toes you step on today might
be connected to the ass youre licking tomorrow

out there at it again
combing the hours watching fish nets run riot
in a makeshift mind where waiters have fled
and made their way home to angry lost wives

out there at it again
and my taste seems to be falling lower with every note sung
as the ice in the glass pretends to make smiling easy
after drinking up a moon taped together in a room
filled with dead poets reciting
clueless prescriptions
armed with flashlights
and a fresh set of batteries

*

and all
is not okay

*

a moment or two later
hurricane sandy belts through
flooding streets
with the latest news flash reporting
the façade of a multi million single home brownstone
on the corner of 14th & 10th
crashed into the sidewalk

thankfully
no one died

*

out there at it again
and like it or not
everyone needs cash
to cope with disaster

so here i am with a bunch of the same
stepping over a shopping cart

filled with smashed beer cans
and a man warm
and roaring with snores
in a secure bank lobby

*

we step over our fear to withdraw
in crisp one hundred dollar bills

*

and yes i can report all of us are smart
and fully aware irony rules the day
in a black out fury

one sin is as good as any other

reggie accepts
one sin is as good as any other

an ongoing poster child
for the police precinct walls

a shot away from becoming
another forgotten shot up star

always on tippy toes
yet unable to dance

or collect before going
straight to jail

reggie licks his lips
and plastic bowl clean

puts his knife back
into his empty back pocket

wishing clocks
could get lost in time

when shopping carts had ash trays
the pharmacy cheap liquor

peeling off a 200lb wound
looking for answers he never questions his maker

wrapped in a paper bag
he might sleep tonight

knowing charity can be a band aid
gnawing at angels

with another no good job
and a half empty bottle of meth

beside a box of bibles
dumped on my doorstep

strange unfriendly places

look at me
look at me
under these glasses
under these shades

look at me
i said look at me
under these glasses
under these shades

there are strange
unfriendly places
where what you look like
really and truly matters

places where
when someone
offers you their hand
and says
you look tired

what they really mean
what they really
truly mean is
fuck me
you are
one ugly
bastard

sticky sweet cactus

sticky sweet cactus
see how she makes me laugh

sigh
and oh so high

showing me the stars
wrapped in chewing gum wrappers

before i am rolled over
in freshly juiced skin

happier than dead flowers
propped on a window ledge

an eclipse with raven hair
falling over my face

fragile as a spider leg
instant as a camera flash

with eyes so deep
they fall apart
a dream catcher web

always giggling
on a borrowed horse

an endless carnival
serenading clowns

tastier than fresh
cut string beans

with a body purely combustible
and constantly in trouble

whistle blower

the poet jams na na beats
across the world wide web

as fear spreads like soggy
peanut butter sandwiches

as maps replace letters
fingers and raw thumbs

carefully cracked then tacked
onto collapsible office walls

creating cell like ears
to track and recreate

prisons of our own
complicated designs

left alone
we can evolve

into monitoring
our own screams

however distant
and predictable

until all that is left becomes
a numb display of passion

punched on ever
reducing keypads

signaling a final rush
to break free again

and with a little luck
learn how to feel

bugs burn in the lamp

bugs burn in the lamp
shadows sleep in their silence

pins and needles
prompt a memory to return

to a time when
much younger than this

i hid underneath
a magnolia tree

the damp grass
stained my jeans

watching apartment lights
flicker on and off

like lost highway signs
redirecting a change in lanes

inviting me to slow down
focus on my intention

before stray dogs
drown out whispers

i can tell she is unaware
i am studying the way

she combs her hair
before an overhead street light
buzzes then explodes

not far from
where i am sitting

cops and ambulances
and fire trucks show up

unfazed
she continues combing

her carpet
of flowing hair

i want to stay
locked in her image

but the fire ants
have found me

us three

us three
deadened by moist misadventure
waking groggy and aware
tomorrow rarely passes

us three
dangling limbs and toes
over weather beaten chairs
retaining youth ever so gradually

us three
yet to prove
acknowledge or lose the idea
we can make it alone together

she
plunging fathoms deep
laced in a fathers
far flung guilt

me
escaping past
a wayward homeland
dispersing thoughts into another cuppa

he
humble host
solid in the silence
and yet all knowing

me
out of touch
dancing with an interior
lampshade mind

she
untactfully placing askew
all of her sixty
thousand odd limbs

me
posing with a light bulb
ready to attack itchy love
with scratchy vinyl interludes

lifer

peeling layers
skin off skin

from unshaven chest
to aching fist

a removable collection
assaults his nerves

a wash away heartbeat
crinkled in knots

what is often unseen
reappears with tears

the handmade pen
the soot and ink

a lit cigarette
signals the ok

watching the smoke
thicken the plot

with a series of tattoos
etched on his chest

telling a story forever
concealed behind bars

the brightest light can shine in the darkest places

this metallic river
tepid and textured
with a mat of mosquito larvae
oil slicks and foaming turds
reports not a ripple
can be seen anywhere

beside this water
i squeeze a dream with possibilities
believing the brightest light
can shine
in the darkest of places

or is it
the darkest light
can shine
in the brightest places

either way
today i am pretending
to be a chemist
rather than
a broken down wordsmith
growing two heads
six bionic lanky limbs
and an assortment
of odd cocks

i so
want to
cool off and jump
into this poisoned quagmire
then reemerge
with the marble eyes
of replenished man

perhaps
grow inwardly
from the experience
closer to insects
or a wild ferocious beast
or morph into something
a little more domesticated
like a baby hedgehog
or a hamster running
on his wheel

*

seems like
i have nothing to loose
and nothing to gain
if my sense of progress
and power to communicate
is reflected in this molten water
suffocated with birth
control pill run off

the worst that can
possible happen
might have
already happened

*

towards
the watery edge
an outdated oxen
waits to be slaughtered
by a unique form
of sanitized
happiness

thalia

a sign i guess
under a broken street light

to stand here for years
and remember the time

when i was honoured
a real fancy uptown statue

now i have to watch
stray dogs piss at my feet

and listen to laughing kids
stick gum up my ass

while deranged punks
spray paint black moustaches

underneath my once delicate
chipped off nose

when dreams are reality

when dreams are reality
and reality the dream
however tormented
sorrow sounds

(unattended baggage
will be removed
and may be destroyed)

there is a fine line
between self pity and loss
some say sadness
i say check the side of
a cereal box
for details

when dreams are reality
and reality the dream
as your hand slips
inside my jeans
in the well used corners
of candle lit shadows
a chorus rings
filled to the brim
reflecting diamonds
on a blood bath moon
with our ever increasing
deceased friends
celebrating and heaving
in the waves whispering
live out all your desires
because no one can tell you
where lost souls weep

crack on

hastings battleground
you gotta love it
four old punks screamed in and inked out
filled with yesterdays adding up to bollocks
torn leather jackets and rusting safety pins

wandering the dizzy streets
with the combined knowledge of well
we are still ere aint we

collapsible exchanges follow
the pages of daze in and out of old haunts
arguing with faded ticket collectors
through nondescription lenses
before scratching at love
in abandoned cars and phone booths

close by shadows of tired women
search for a few tired old men

back in the late seventies
when political bullies came and went
it was a battle alright
booze juiced with anarchy
the energy of not caring adding up
to half pissed expressions
that somehow connected frustrations
giving a voice for change
doomed because it dare try

laughing at all the skills we used up
seems almost justifiable

yet in these quiet moments
watching the tide turn

i can still breathe with the fire
pop a pill if i want
take a shot or more
trying to figure out
what it is all about

yes here we all are here again
making the rounds in this sea swept town
with a cackle of mods and rockers
hiding in the corners of middle age
cheering ex punks reading out dated poems
roaring with authentic despair

give me a twenty someone yells
and let us talk about it later

i hide in their creased faces
caress scars from broken pint glasses

the smell of cheap curry haunts
the burnt nostrils of stray dogs
prowling this wind wept promenade
while clean cut bobbies
do their clean cut next right thing
and tempt me to believe no one cares
because no one appears to be judging

inspired arm in arm
the moon seems tougher
than your new tattoo

before missing the last train
back to the pin striped smog
as another wave recedes
as we pace with screeching gulls
in search of scraps for memories
and bits of disfigured memorabilia

to fill up sand covered notebooks
with the craving there must be
fresh answers loitering
if nothing else
close by

zippo slaves

crows squawk of love
besieged on park benches

layers of buttocks and half expressed torsos
sweat and peel with blistered skin

on this side of a locked up summer green
inside a broken syringe

pigeons peck on pigeons
rummaging through a trash pile

his ex imagines everything to be a reflection
viewed thru flames and exploding gas

her ex quotes bar numbers and wake up calls
from mothers and a flock of dead sisters

whose clocks have stopped way past free condoms
ozone layers and compulsory urine samples

ode to blakes mandible

oh miasma sipping
gazing into a petro glyphic wing
motion begins with colour
through the locked keyholes
of way too many seething things

human tissue
in the pastel clinic
bare bulb light
paces with lough like limbs
cross examining
the promise of higher beings

the living outnumber
the living dead
a recent tax audit read

leaving me to inspect
shadows and scriptures
scratched with shards of glass
in search of clues to overcome
the maggots endless yawn

without words

without words she says i see nothing
except a distorted world laced in endless bills
odd chairs and a damp book of matches
stuffed behind a flea bitten sofa

without words he says i feel nothing
needs to be shared or cherished or sung
except a mortgaged house with dishwasher soap
unable to clean a room compromised with aches and pains

without words you say i feel like the sick
the stranded the used and undone
marine sitting beside us trying to forgive
a bomb lodged inside his brain

skin mates

skin mates

skin mates
forget the poisoned rain and pc bees
arm in arm let us head on past the deserted railway tracks
past the dripping wires transporting madness
hand in hand let us wade through soft lily fields
and dance on lush red trumpet creepers
for the wedding lawns have been cut and sterilized
the golf courses flushed and trimmed
and our bellies are stuffed with seedless watermelon flesh

let us run through open pastures rolling in cloud cover
resembling exploding faces with ever widening screams
sea horses and cosmic orgies
dissolving the armies of barbed wire posted signs
blocking our escape from gulp buster trash
and the constant need for more

echo skin mates echo

you who are the shadows of my youth
resembling dizzy swaggering pirates
seeking a plank on a sinking ship
continually attached like a syringe in a weak vein
a thousand years from now may your faces shine
in opaque skies filled with restless whispers
above lettuce clouds
crisscrossing a thousand suns

may your photocopied fingerprints
travel like bone biblical chaff
along the elite corridors of greed
burying an avalanche of profiteering
and moronic warmongers
laced in chicken thin skins
thriving on humanities blisters

oh harmless freaks
floating belly up
our reflections fear nothing
after all the toxins inside this pond
equal the toxins inside us all

or have you grown deaf
to the church bells chiming
how unclean we have always been

skin mates
remember the gas masks
for the ceremony of fire
scorches the healthiest lungs
before sending us sliding into quicksand
manufactured from bloody classrooms
draped in caution tape and unending
weather forecasts

and yet
even though i am limp
heavy and heaving
waiting for a quick pick me up
to sweep me back into my boots
i write these words for you
beside this contaminated pond

you who can barely consume
you who wear the hard hats
the dirty aprons and rubber gloves
the dust masks and bus drivers
the rubber maid angels and cleanup crews
the nurses and teachers
the aliens born on this planet
aching to be reborn
no longer torn or disguised
or worse insulted and bombarded

by fabricated ailments and wars
venom induced cures
resulting in the wasted hours of apathy and bloodshed
symbolizing the worst form of treachery

skin mates
before the ink runs out
may my pink sticky flesh
laugh at the raw scratching
as i lay here open like a wound
flaunting my faults
stained with glue
on a quest for new songs
found in an oil stained turtle shell
placed against your fragile ear

oh sad country of my bones

oh
sad
country
of my bones
swift dragonflies
fill the red molten sky
my wires ache from riding
on the polished pebbles of time
nerves connect to the motion
of signage and revelations
as cats purr on laps
as an angel unties
her muddy boots
to find me
here

rah
through time
rah through these lines
no crime is greater
than loves
abuse

the sun
is asking
which way
are you truly
lost

notice
my shadows
have left the fields
as you return to a wounded house
childlike and knowing you have stolen
another secret glimpse

of lifes revolving
perfection

i
am
not
guilty
as a thief
when i run
to avoid hiding
in the sweaty
tears of regret
knowing my soul
will keep me
warm

i
am
not guilty
when i steal
because i feel
the stinging bee
or hear the faint
flutter of a
falling
leaf

&
once
again

the
moon
asks me
which way
oh sad country
of my bones

will you dare
continue to travel
if you are truly
lost

without
strict direction
and a shipmates compass
the noise and energy of confusion
contain the knowledge to make or break
an outburst of passion looking
at an unfinished canvas
in a state of endless
mystery

oh
sad country
of my bones
be grateful
i can say i will
never see or feel
more than enough
at least for today
at least until
death begins
to cry

hit
out with
a clenched fist
bruising bloody flesh
on a cold concrete wall
clogged up with
my mind out
of control
again

oh
sad country
of my bones
no crime is greater
than loves
abuse

rah
through time
rah through these
long and languid
lines

i step
outside
and under a
leaking awning roll
another cigarette

blowing burnt ash onto tepid ink

through a maze of shuffling
fingers rummage deep
within ashtray isles

convinced one more 4am
buried in this corner on dartmoor
with bugs and lamplight
can help understand
a broken backed teacher
dusting chalk dust scars
in a world selling
how lucky we are
to an empty class room

between sighs and swigs
he sputters how tired
not enough living
has become

across fields laced
with fresh gravel and tar
sirens wail as they approach
a car and mangled badger

staring at the peeling ceiling
he tries to forget all of the above
through a maze of torn paper
burnt with tepid black ink

i chart these poems onto your skin

i chart these poems onto your skin
shimmering petals dancing in a swirl

forming a labyrinth of novae and pulsars
before daylight fades into a draco smile

kaleidoscope dreams awaken calm
inbetween seconds these scissors are sharp
the ink on this bill
forms a fist
attached to these eyes
a pendulum drops

long after the wick has lost its way
without a sound veins untangle
hollow out the horn
unlock the gate

climb from freeing breath
to slip through wire and unhook the lure

night unfolds a ptolemaic flame
and cadmus rises to chart these poems to begin again

later

rocking back and forth
you say regret is a coward
written all over my face

my general lack of history
cow horns
rocking red roosters
sick to the stomach
wants to suck on someone else
for change

crow moon is full
and black and hollow
reach for a knife
cut open a tomato

*

without seals
and rings and dogs

what an unhealthy lot we are
spock necker

*

it sucks realizing death
has a shot at spinning life out of control

shadow

shadow
when i cry
you cry
when i speak
you listen
what i see
you see
what i feel
you soothe

shadow
when the wind blows
you move not
when the rain falls
you stay dry
when the sun shines
some say
we grow

shadow
when the bombs drop
you stay unharmed
when i am told how to live
you laugh
when i speak
you listen
when the crowd breaks
you stay
when love exits
you return
when i am here
you are near
when i am in trouble
you remain the same

disco donny

we are all going to party
you beamed
3000 of your closest friends
all on the guest list

disco donny
you were a legend
to every raver
south of the mason dixie border
with your sky melting diamonds
and sequin studded suits
flashing your pirate smile
across gigantic screens
flickering in details
and fast beat milky ways

with the confused beauty of angels
a sea of post teen torsos
perfect and plastic
swayed in your presence
until daybreak dared to reappear

their torn clothes removed
their party animalistic minds
infested in love storms
ensuring this scene remained
six feet underground

on day glow silver sprayed wings
crowds unwrapped their souls for you
tweaking in unreachable unknowns
forever dancing
in between heaven and hell

with you the grand puppeteer
feeding electrocuted pulses
and etching their minds
to explore never to be found again
universes cascading
in overloaded wonder

squiggles in the rain

burning a parting hour
to board a distant train

there you are again
squiggles in the rain

traceless questions
rekindling a muddy flame

i have written she said
danced and bled for you

gained memories
some were large

others
far too small

some move quickly
others too slow

and many felt as if
nothing ever happened at all

yet none of this is
as transparent as these

squiggles in the rain

uncrossing her legs
she wipes her lips

you on me she says
and me in you

is kind of like hot blisters
burning in the sand

can we try again
i ask out the window

look she smiles
the train is moving

yet we sit
still and cold

i can change
i lie

al green is playing on the radio

fleeting shadows follow
the tattoos over your skin

across cheap paneled walls
onto the motel floor

concerned conversations about decorating
street lamps with woolen scarfs

and elevating churches
wash out the night

another appointment has ended
without balloons

*

back inside distorted raindrops
touch burnt fingers

dipped in tangled hair
beside the mirrored glass

images
dismantle themselves

and where reflections melt
you sigh in relief

after the door slammed shut
feeling his presence leave

*

through a slit in a crumpled blind
you pray like a ghost for nothing more

aware with luck for the very last time
his anger shall never return to leave you

crawling back
into your skin

back into the medicine cabinet
with no place else to go

meditating on the toilet seat
to a choir of tampons crushed towels and mushy soap

your beating heart wants to be left alone
with al green playing on the radio

*

the damp chill blowing in through the cracks
feels comforting on shaved legs and freshly painted toes

all this belongs to me you smile
slipping on a tight dress and half cut bra

a new seamless thong
a pair of silver polished boots

what is gone is gone
you hum believing a reckless gesture

doing the same thing differently
again and again

can change your life
forever

overdose

Overdose

Poets argument

*Perhaps the strangest action surviving a drug overdose
is rather than being overwhelmed with an initial sense of gratitude for being alive
a cloud of remorse and self-loathing linger.
Negativity led to a state of depression both physical and mental
best described as a blanket smothering out light.*

*Trapped in a corner of my own design
I accepted the blanket's smothering advances
Until drawing a knife
sliced the coarse fabric into wincey pieces.*

*With the ripped fabric on fire
I asked the grinning inevitable to go elsewhere to reap
and the poet to Mystery.*

*20 something odd years ago
words began weaving themselves onto napkins and scrap paper.
20 something years later surviving the flood waters of Hurricane Katrina
little changed in their arrangement.*

*Thanks to lighter fluid and friendship
Overdose is a blanket burning*

*Asking words to fly from their cages
across uncharted seas
towards the many who never ever
swim back.*

overdose

the labyrinth inevitable grins
voices snarl

we told you so
dumbass

panic explodes into torrential remorse
leaving an ongoing journey unable to connect

and disconnect
this is all there is

until remembering not a thing
before a stretcher enters charity hospital

before this emergency room becomes a womb
before remembering words scribed in a mist

resemble spilt seconds passing as shadows
gliding over granite lichen and badger teeth

remembering
i am unable to connect the dots

from 20 odd years nestled in the rocky cavities of time
to 20 years later becoming an abstraction

extracted into an ultrabright landscape
moulded from play dough

remembering crows screeching
spat out gullies streams charged with fish

remembering your bare feet
giggling in the river tavy

overdose as if upon your command
best described as senseless and stoned

a state of perpetual being is replaced with wires
sticky cords and tubes filled with gluey petroleum jelly

expertly attaching themselves to a convulsing frame
with a brain unconvinced if returning

back into the divide
is in anyway necessary

knowing failed bravado has retreated
into the dependency of others

paramedics nurses doctors cops and porters
all giving with their jobs

all human enough to ignore
my unsigned puzzle of vomit

this is it bucko i blob
defecating my jeans

before every remembered word
designed to cut into the brain

becomes a strangers voice
fusing a force with life

shivering in
90 degrees

overdose

like waves bulling their way through
gobs of foam to reach then recede

like branches twisted and brittle
snapping burnt hair across a field

pure voltage
humming in the shallows

overdose your fever
refracts into splinters

mingling with a numb buzzing
under an array of digits and light

choirs of hands with sterilized gloves
expertly prodding to keep whats left alive

and in the inbetween
seconds when the festering tomb

climbs through the spine
clogged arteries shake

before fading out again
with electricity singing hair

overdose

i admit i am convinced
with a mouth stuffed with tubes

reciting sacred oaths
memorized like grocery lists

once pinned to a door
before seconds later

heart starts
beating

an inner mantra deafening
the tired cops ear

his warm hand
holds mine as i slip back

both knowing death smells
the stench of burnt living flesh

overdose leaves me for words
like sorry for wasting so much of your time

without pain a fresh needle
misses a vein

whats that burning smell
i ask the nurse politely

before squeezing stone
before bits and pieces cram themselves

into a self forced to remember who
or what i have now become

through a fuzzy field of monitors
a doctor laughs youre one lucky bastard

there was enough dope in you
to refuel our pharmacy

overdose fades into a mixture of silt and slime
wishing for a pen to write anything except any of this down

hoping words can make this all disappear
and banish questions mangled in destiny

overdose
words
ebb

towards a sold out emergency ward
where people are really dying

their dying feels different
their dying feels real

perhaps from living a shitty life
a little too fast

perhaps unable to recognize
what we are often dealt with

requires a lot more
than love

overdose
words
flow

look around at this
sold out emergency ward

i feel selfishly alive
superficially unplugged

my death over exposed
next to gunshot wounds

amputated limbs
diabetic seizures

car wrecks
miscarriages

my death feels
inadequate and too easy

a sloppy joke
wasting a place in eternity

as if accepting the stone
cold lip of the grave

appears nothing more
than an insurance adjuster

wearing mirror shades

overdose why do so many pass
before you unnoticed

hours move the mind
resetting regret into tears

gooey puddles
on plastic sheets

my mate appears concerned
hes here to check on his investment

he recedes into
a pair of overgrown hands

behind a clinical mask
im asked if i can stop scratching

and no i cannot leave this hospital
for now says the mask

let this drip replace
shards of glass

overdose i ask
never to sleep with you again

before the monkey on my back
fumbles for my shirt

before stumbling off a gurney
checking the wallet

before hailing a cab
before scoring from the driver

before returning to a cage
to focus on baggage

long ago forgotten
yet somehow

never left
behind

now where

bits of him woke
while other bits remain afloat

half asleep in a cold sweat
under the sheets laced with wasted words

he finds a thumbnail sketch made of her
from her who else

in time he searched with hands on knees
fingers sifting insect like through dust and rubble
in the corners of forgotten cracks
for anything passing as liquid colour

remembering how a face
made every shadow dance

in the still born swamp place
where palmettos grow and herons soar
into a space they both call home

impossible star

buttonhole eyes
unlock the door
late last night and night before
snow fell keeping silent
the shock tethered inside
hours passing as a heartbeat

*

on an expanse of horizon
found lost in central park
walking without direction
hands clenched in pockets

an inner scream believes
you are warmer elsewhere
frozen with burning snow

*

crossing soho
a rainbow shines and drips

in a forgotten garden
cultivated in need of serenity
beneath the knees
footprints sink in puddles

*

wiping away brittle leaves
taxi horns echo past

on store front windows
reflections ask what landscape is this
now the glitter has faded

the sacred drizzle of acceptance

tonight charging phones
animated frogs dance over the screen

what is it about humans
she asks the dancing frogs

alive we stumble through life
desperately trying not to weep or be upset

and yet crying and anger can be
the most healing of actions

creating a force
to feed new life

like that crazy preacher
who stands in the middle of the street

every sunday
shaking his fists at heaven

singing and crying
whoosh amen

whoosh amen
i ask

silence
before you clear your throat

no not really
you reply

look honey i say forget the frogs
are we actually here having a conversation

funny you say that
being the oh so sensitive kinda guy

like cursed sisyphus forever pushing a boulder
up his own manmade hill

whatever happened to keep on
holding and never letting go

what are you talking about
you know what

it is written in clear audible text
all over your squirming face

what does it spell i am unhinged
lost in the sacred drizzle of acceptance

exact size

tonight there is only a few bellies to feed
in this ruin of a takeout diner

things are slow enough
the waitress can prep the coleslaw

exact size is important when it comes to her carrots
cabbages and onions

i am shaking in the kitchen
washing out an empty pickle jar fit for recycling

it is one of those large economy size jars
you can buy from any super store

the brain of a president could fit inside that jar
she laughs mixing in the mayonnaise

i admit the way she smiles and handles a knife
reminds me of my mom and to be honest

the only reason i stay
working in this dump

from the beginning

from
the beginning
before we recognized
the silence of time slipping
and the quotations on a black board
seemed to make a whole lot more sense
before stepping outside to gaze glazed
at the miracle of the rising moon
before the first drop of water
sprinkled on our heads
there were tears
drying on
broken
skin

before
the thrill of
a mystery novel
sent us running into
misplaced adventures
before the waves breaking on
this shore reminded me to ask
the ocean if she ever tires
of taking the lost souls
of hardy men

before
fishermen
repairing their nets
recount mermaid visions
there were tears
drying on
broken
skin

from
the beginning
in the silent memories
of simple things shared like
brushes dipped in the same paint can
or hand shadows dancing on a
ceiling inside a screen porch
or depicting flowers
stubborn and alive
blooming in
this frigid
winter

there were tears
drying on
broken
skin

before
a half empty
cup of coffee spills
creating a shallow pool
evaporating somewhere between
a shadow morphing sunlight
and the shape of you dying
there were tears
drying on
broken
skin

before
clouds made
dragons and demons
before i rejected laughter
for the contents found inside
this busted open suitcase
revealing a sack of bones

i never stop holding
there were tears
drying on
broken
skin

bombs are dropping there

bombs are dropping there
stomachs crunch here

can anyone explain
which one is fucking life

*

ever woken she said
after dreaming the night awake

or slept fully clothed
under the skins naked heart

last night two commercials collided
soaked and stained reel to real

your on my tongue she said again
in the mouths moonlit mind

this cigarette is useless
this pill a fumble

*

stepping outside
raining a three day smile

with outstretched hands
this flower is for your hair you say

this blood stained t shirt
wiping my inner thigh

be thankful
all mine

*

where we are

awake from where we have come from
bones feel cleansed in the revealing freshness

wet granite glistens like stars on a tent
as cool mountain air ripples across this lake

your boots shine in the sunlight
forming footprint beginnings in dewdrop fields

an impulse to return into the unknown
pushes us forward inside a daydream

safe as snails
constant yet changing

you are in me and vice versa
together for now crawling inside one shell

past the lessons time taught us
hand in hand we can forget how to die

cake walk

the last televised man
to walk on the moon

forgot to apologize
for being late

beneath the skin

deep shadows line these empty pockets
on a night frozen still with silent snow

a companion owl surveys his rodent wares
displaying claws of deathly precision

above the clouds hidden stars
embrace the storm and keep me warm

keeps what is left of my soul to return
to words flowing through swollen veins

offering comfort as i chip away
with cigarettes and smoke

quickening to burn
these unmoving movements

laced in wonder
and fueled with fleeting time

*

many miles and heartbeats away
images send me without sail or compass

into a sea of falling hair
where i drown in the pulse of our beating hearts

sinking into a place where hands and lips
are released and free to caress the fire

found deep beneath the skin

hanging with quasimodo vultures

plucking fires out of the crypt
in search of fluffy balls of cotton
we find a spoon in a messed up kitchen

over the walls someone scrawled
broken needles never rust
in damp echoes of forgotten corners

hanging with quasimodo vultures
i recognize youth can end dead ending
with hammered joe and noddy bickering
without a twist of lime

minutes forget to learn
and long before then
joe barks at noddy coughing blood
can you move your lily white ass and assist

lifting a warm beer can off a beer warm belly
into a beer worn mouth
in the negative nodding noddy nods back no

is this all you two can do i barely spark
aware decay is morphing with a bug riddled carpet

i can switch bad habits like a chameleon noddy scoffs
quicker than a hyena can change a pair of diapers blurts joe
or for that matter
faster than you can paint them

paint what i bark propping up a sink
a new set of spots what else joe blurs
at the minutes forgetting to learn how often
time forgets to move on
as we pass out again

keep on keeping on

the poet with potential
oscillates back and forth

on the same arc
hoping each swing

and every word uttered
will not be the last

before gravity conquers
and the pendulum stops

a slash of reddish polka dots

are you ready to wake up
no not really
can i stay like this for
a slice of eternity

not that my dreams amount to so much anymore
just a slash of reddish polka dots
spotting the sheets

*

i thought you were up for
melting with the shadows

maybe slip and slide over the sidewalk
in laced up boots

*

i am
yet where

*

coincidences feel distorted
whenever i try to retrace the facts

*

outside soggy news
floats thru the streets

power lines sway
with edible sounds

you shrink too much
you continue clutching herbal tea

if it wasnt for me you would forget
how often i remind you how often

you are always
forgetting to eat

an omen of sorts

drawn nearer with time
naked and exhausted

strangers last night somehow by morning
their bodies ache for more

a bird flies through an open window
across their heads hitting the lamp

panics and flusters
before flying outside again

an omen of sorts she says
something about travel and good luck

*

under the winter sun
leaves search upwards

i turn inwards
wanting to scale your body

a smile can travel many uncharted miles
you say pulling down the blinds

let us journey backwards
to where we are now

close the screen door
leave the key under the flowerpot

let laughter
melt this frigid snow

far rockaway beach

dropped out of the sky
a seagull lands on far rockaway beach
distorted now from hurricane sandy

brittle winds throw raw diamonds
across the cheeks of broken faces

torn clothes and curtains cling to
barbed wire fences

folks are freezing
without heat or homes

thanks hurricane katrina
i can help this time

batteries
flashlights
tampons
blankets
bandages
gas heaters
heavy coats
condoms
a christmas tree

*

rummaging thru rotting paper
i descend into the fragile

carrion join the gulls in endless pecking
as a different world unveils

firefighters and cops
utility workers and volunteers

wading thru pulp fiction
with an ability to hug survivors

and absorb
endless tears

*

on rain drenched jackets
katrina clings tireless

like these clothes
and busted refrigerators

blistering heat freezing fear
to shiver i scratch with endless seagull pecking

enough will never do

desire laced with electricity
towered through blistered thoughts
like two glazed cherries rolled over ice
they melted out of taxis
the last to arrive always
the first thrown out

you devoured fingernails grappling with belt buckles
i roared bloated watching manhattan melt in a rain

a stranger commented on how well the drugs were doing
before noticing the razors in your eyes
need more than a steam bath to unglue
churning stomachs and choking conversations
strung out on broken telephone cords
reflected in the frozen snow

*

sharp teeth surround us
cuddling the stains of red wine
as we decipher hidden messages
scattered on the subway ceiling

with a punch you nicknamed ratmando
our lives felt glued together buzzing in neon
before i quoted how you resemble a twig
dancing on a bumble bee sting

*

below the barbed wire railings
someone has scrawled

fillets from heaven heave
all kinds of manner
invisible destinations leave apples

whipped in woollen socks
what does it all mean
you asked as ted the egg arrived
tapping his fingernails like a crow beak
tapping a frosted glass

i say will you look at that ted smiles
towards the infinite skyline
the billboards have stopped singing
now the new mayor moved in

and no amount of reason
can help us understand why
we have to invent a new form of sign language

mark up and down my words he continued
it will not be long before overpriced persona will isolate
according to their own beliefs
and when that moment arrives in silence
on every street corner we will finally realize
we consume our own trash

a few blocks later
out of breath on silent communion
it can be tricky to notice how
feelings become itemized
beneath black stockings
with savannah silk legs

*

time hiccups on
two cold punctured bodies
lost beneath branches bitten through by winter
huddle under the covers and forget to undress

something smells fried she says at last
enough will never do
holding my cock for ransom

holding hands

stains on our shoes
slip off the flooded sidewalk

distorting where we have traveled
with steps yet taken

*

edible colours suggest
birds seem to be digesting

a lighter way of living
in limbs of broken trees

backfire

open the door and deepen the questions
let the bell ringer ring her truth

heal a knife wound as scars of past lives
cut confusion along murky landscapes
where hidden costs backfire into whimpers scratching
a smoked out moon

*

watch the muralist on wet gravel paint
a traveling show for unforgiving hands

without clues found on twitter or facebook
ghosts scale a barbed wire fence
before rescuing post dated smiles

no matter what

no matter what was said
they woke to find the world wordless

rain fell silent and self seeking
realized a mute stare

cracking the vanity mirror
with lipstick you scrawled

the butterflies escaped
without their wings

buried alive

buried alive
in past reminders
he threw away
sets of disillusions

*

using a paper clip
like they do in the movies
the lock got picked
then fled into the familiar

*

without regret
the shovel broke
knowing a mad badger
chases his own tail

laced in splinters

bound knowing
this is the last round
laced in splinters
and bits of broken time
the bottle finishes long before
hidden stars spangle
in a floor of broken glass

*

reeking with a whiff of fame
convinced blood may have been poisoned
from risky forgotten handshakes
forced to conclude an exit plan is needed
without a tent or gun
part jew part gentile
fights a delicate balance
jumbled up scowling

*

napkin doodles dance between
crimes committed and the wise fool
slouched arguing how
cash in empty pockets
rarely makes any sense
except to stretch out odd hours
before straitening up
to connect the dots and accept
there is little peace to be found in
the simple gifts contrived as humility

make the distance

wanting to be more than interchangeable
armed with less than perfect

beyond the rooftop horizon
fires burn on the levees

an orange mist settles on the commerce of day
begging the question how much further
can a blind man see

senses awakened to the prowling night
continue to flicker in the never fading sell out
making the distance between shooting stars and streets
a self induced blessing or a service for hire curse

either which way when hot fires burn cold
through fractured smiles and throw away grins

on the verge of being
on the verge of seeing

after so many wars i have to ask
if our eyes are the keys to our souls
where is the lock
and who dare be the locksmith

all that floats feels raw

all that floats feels raw

delaune quietly knows
we flood towards the sea
and if lucky enough

return silent
with a tide resembling
dust on a mantle

*

nails pulled from the wall
take away something
no longer deemed important

the lightning behind
caked streaked blinds
breaks above the roof line

*

through the fireworks
found in blood shot eyes
worlds appear distorted

trees resemble cities
submerged mountains
vast blocks of industry

*

buckled river banks recede
and in this leftover night
at any given moment

we sense an inner memory
can slay us into believing again
all that floats feels raw

he began to notice

he began to notice the same blank faces
reflecting over shot up street signs

stray dogs and cats mingled with sirens
an array of crushed stars dazzled

the fried chicken shack next door
filled senses with fat fried chicken

*

underneath a blooming magnolia tree
he kicked over a mop bucket and snapped a broom

before scurrying along street car tracks
bewildered and backpedaling a lifetime of schemes

running always running
back into the audubon hotel

he checked into a tomb sighing
out there oh lordy lordy

is by far with little doubt
way too weird

outside harrys

what if love has no cure
what if the familiar is also true

this place feels oh so white
can we reload and start again

what are the chances this snow cannot melt
what if the details are rarely important

can smiles deny breaking glass
reflecting through magnolia trees

what if these memories can reshape a heart
and a frozen carrot replace my busted nose

geese huddle in a valley further north
forgotten berries cling to the vine

what if this suitcase contained a song
and my gloves stay hidden under your car seat

the evening cascades into silence
a sunset dazzles buttons for eyes

what if stars look upon this place
yet headless questions continue to bicker and wait

when need is translated into needing more
no text or message can pull the trigger

what happens when footprints resemble ashes
and a distant song drifts into space

a nest of ravens weaves through your hair
this borrowed torn scarf itches my chin

what if ultimatums are rarely important
as icy sweat clings in a state of slow motion

heavy you echo
is a new breed of word

crawling back into itself

like snails lost without shells
reload reload plays russian roulette
on the backs of broken tracks

beside a hotel pool a camera crew
films selfies as spandex bodies
with tattooed skulls dangle
crawling back into themselves

*

on a shelf in the shop lifters room
so many wise words meander in dust
glued to worthless wrappers
along cut up rails we read

fear preys on bowing heads
hoping this world will always be
crawling back into itself

*

soggy notes and faded photographs
once stuck on overstuffed refrigerators
float between her legs

in a city drowned beyond recognition
reflecting a world some say
will always be crawling back into itself

a world on fire

*

a world on fire
yr last text read

nails on a mortgaged cross
grow rusty with rage

bombs are served over easy
onto digitalized screams

and i am on ice
wading through rhubarb

*

nightmares are no longer
a frayed mathematical problem

crows are cawing madness
across a boiling sea bed

the moon lost an eye kissing
a bruised sons shadows

i have a sharp knife
and a bushel of rhubarb

*

reports across the wire
hail a resurrected dead head

outplays a drone
through an optical stream

friends riot in london town
now they have read the ballot

and yours truly is washing rhubarb
in a galvanized sink

*

28 days of hatha yoga
resulted in a twelve pack of guinness

the magnetic letters on the fridge
misspelled what if

some say the devil is weeping
trying to choose our next president

the neutrals remain home sick
swallowing sacks stuffed with hemp

and with a spoonful of honey
i boil rhubarb

*

the organic fireworks are soggy
after skinny dipping in a swamp

the great wall of china recently sold
to a cattle rancher in texas

refugees can apply for free tickets
one way to pluto

as i strain rhubarb
through a rusty clogged up sieve

*

the neighbors busy writing grants
to prop up diabetic limbs

hamburgers on the grill resemble
a chorus of bats in heat

independence day has renamed itself
co dependence for all

thankfully the rhubarb is in the freezer
and the cats are well fed

*

not much else to report
since i last read your text

the world is on fire
at least i think that is what you meant

late again yet feeling early

as always i am late again
yet feel uncannily early

with a pocket of broken pencils
ready to draw a round of blanks

too many invisible words
make deciphering impossible

everyday visons rarely equate to
love at first sight

your well worn smile
perplexes my frown

strapped to a capsule
everything tastes fresh

lost pages stay clean
unlike these boots

we all know puddles reflect
a vague misunderstanding

there is little chance to reconnect
she wailed after the meltdown

so many flags wanting
to share so little sky

with nothing to add
i disappeared quick enough

too many hands firing
the same round of bullets

tomorrows old news

tonight we huddle
where we have stood before
after the burial after another long haul
wearing white knuckled emotions
shaking hands strung out on limbs

saving what we know for an unknown date
as yet another debate tries to save the day
with a pack of wet matches

waiting in line
wound tight with obsolete things
the suitcase bursts open
only to reveal how not to pack
anymore reasons to cry or ask why

he reads if i had a choice
or the chance to choose
you my love would be a cello
gift wrapped and stored
behind bullet proof glass
occasionally played
in the thundering rain
by an emaciated musician
with willow like fingers
and a storm of godmothers

yes if i had a choice
or the chance to choose
no orchestral accompaniment
or choir like ensemble
could join us together
on this disheveled sidewalk
where the damaged and undone
rain drenched with the shivers

somehow keep on going
with their mangled lives
buried beneath soggy sheets
of tomorrows old news

another stinger down

and the boy the world called all of a sudden
seems to have straightened most of himself out

standing and waving a friendly gesture
the new neighbours are moving in with yoga mats

he is convinced what happened last night in the bedroom
belongs to a game of chance regardless of rules

disillusionment lays in wait like a flea or worse a tick
ready to picnic on what is left

a text message says no way can he go back to precisely this
or that lost time unless luck changes hands

unconvinced elton john pipes through the bus station
translating a childhood with fresh vinyl smells

he so wanted to meet bernie yet knew the odds were stacked
for a dyslexic punk in south east london

after asking his father what does getting laid actually mean
in his cloistered study filled with ancient books

written in hebrew greek and latin
dedicated to another poet speaking his truth

dedicated to another poet
chances are he will never meet

token

meditate in the moment
breathe inner calm

a mist finds the mountain lake
silent before dawn

we glide you whisper
with effervescence glittering

on a pair of translucent
dragonfly wings

travelling the distance between pen and ink

sing
how lips quicken
moments traveling
the distance between
pen and ink
and back again

wrap ribbons around
makeshift resolutions
crossed out maybes
where the hell are you
and come back soon

repeat
how deranged i am
when dark eyes lack your smile
my tongue your skin

believe
in the pillow silence
with a tendency to pace
sleepless and shivering
before returning
after returning from
all the way out there

someone other than me

someone
other than me
keeps us safe
in the rough daze of light
beating thru busted
drawn shades
offering answers
to confuse me further

someone
other than me
circulates outside
in a fevered pitch
on a daily basis
sweeping the steps
and cooking eggs
with no end in sight

someone
bigger than me
sweats and blows
and forces through
the rain sleet and snow
picking up the trash
outside my door

and whoever you are
i write these words
to thank you

www.ingramcontent.com/pod-product-compliance
Lightning Source LLC
Chambersburg PA
CBHW031142160426
43193CB00008B/219